Advance Praise for *Mo[dern Kinship]*

"*Modern Kinship* is the book that LGBT[Q Christians have been wait]ing for. David and Constantino Khalaf take on imp[ortant and] taboo topics with both wisdom and vulnerability. Offering direction and hope to a marginalized group of people who have long been left out of marriage discussions, *Modern Kinship* not only validates the unions of LGBTQ couples but helps them last and thrive. I am grateful to finally have a resource for those who need life-giving advice on how to make their marriage last."

—Amber Cantorna, National Speaker and Author of *Unashamed: A Coming-Out Guide for LGBTQ Christians* and *Refocusing My Family*

"In this much-needed book, David and Constantino Khalaf take the conversation around same-sex relationships in the church beyond apologetics, offering practical insight and wisdom for LGBTQ Christians seeking to find their way in the world of dating, love, sex, and marriage, all too often without the family and community support they deserve. Through their writing, the Khalafs also show how the faithful witness of same-sex Christian couples can enrich and inform the practice and understanding of marriage for all Christians, regardless of sexual orientation."

—Matthew Vines, Executive Director of The Reformation Project and author of *God and the Gay Christian: The Biblical Case in Support of Same-Sex Relationships*

"David and Constantino Khalaf have given the LGBTQ Christian community several gifts. Together, they have taken years to work through some of the most crucial conversations and challenges facing an LGBTQ couple who may be seriously dating, engaged, or even newly married. David and Tino, thoughtful relationship leaders, have now compiled their wisdom and experiences in this much-needed book. Marriage counseling is often unavailable for LGBTQ Christian couples. In its lieu, David and Tino have created an effective tool that encourages couples to have productive conversations about engagement and wedding plans, fidelity, family, and children. Their book truly is a gift."

—Kathy Baldock, Executive Director of Canyonwalker Connections and author of *Walking the Bridgeless Canyon: Repairing the Breach between the Church and the LGBT Community*

"Christians are overdue for a marriage resource that is intentionally inclusive across all sexual orientations. *Modern Kinship* is an instant classic, helpful to couples of any arrangement—including straight folks."

—Mike McHargue, Host of *Ask Science Mike* and Cofounder of *The Liturgists*

"Couples in same-sex marriages have few places to turn to, and even fewer public examples, for modern, wise counsel on what it takes to build a healthy relationship that will last. *Modern Kinship* has arrived just in time. New information for and about same-sex committed relationships was the least of all the gifts I received from reading this book. This book brought me a new perspective on faith, fidelity, and what it really means to be a family. I'm thrilled to be able to have something to offer same-sex couples who are looking for practical ways to build a life they love."
— Michelle Peterson, Author of *#staymarried: A Couple's Devotional* and Cohost of *The #staymarried* podcast

"This book goes deep. Dave and Tino invite us to think deeply, no matter our relationship status, and ask the question: What does it mean to bring our full selves to our intimate relationships? Their stories of dating, navigating sexual ethics, working with shame, and figuring out how to do marriage as a gay Christian couple are full of hard-won wisdom. *Modern Kinship* is as practical as it is inspiring; it gives me great hope."
— Matthias Roberts, Host of *Queerology: A Podcast on Belief and Being*

"I can't think of a better book when it comes to helping kinfolk in and around our church find belonging, purpose, and love available to all of us! Jesus invited us to embrace the kingdom of God that was among all of us. The Khalafs offer just that to those LGBTQ friends pursuing Christian marriage and allies supporting them along the way."
— Adam Nicholas Phillips, Founding Pastor of Christ Church: Portland

"As a pastor who was trained on a conservative theology, my only knowledge of romantic relationships was based on cisgender heteronormativity. So when our son came out, we had no vision of what a nonhetero relationship would look like. As I've gotten to know Dave and Tino, they have helped me see the beauty of what I had never seen. Their stories removed much of the fears I had for my gay son by undoing the harmful stereotypes that I was brought up with. And I'm thankful that I now finally have a book that I can recommend to queer Christian couples. But the importance of this book is not limited to only queer couples; it is invaluable for parents of queer children who have little understanding of what a healthy, romantic, queer relationship looks like."
— Pastor Danny Cortez, Founder of Estuary Space

Modern Kinship

A Queer Guide
to Christian Marriage

DAVID AND CONSTANTINO KHALAF

WESTMINSTER
JOHN KNOX PRESS
LOUISVILLE · KENTUCKY

First edition
Published by Westminster John Knox Press
Louisville, Kentucky

19 20 21 22 23 24 25 26 27 28—10 9 8 7 6 5 4 3 2

Unless otherwise indicated, Scripture quotations are from the New Revised Standard Version of the Bible, copyright © 1989 by the Division of Christian Education of the National Council of the Churches of Christ in the U.S.A., and are used by permission.

Scripture taken from *The Message*, copyright © 1993, 1994, 1995, 1996, 2000, 2001, 2002. Used by permission of NavPress Publishing Group. Represented by Tyndale House Publishers, Inc., Carol Stream, Illinois 60188. Scripture quotations noted CEB are taken from the Common English Bible, copyright 2011. Used by permission. All rights reserved.

Book design by Drew Stevens
Cover design by Mark Abrams

Library of Congress Cataloging-in-Publication Data
Names: Khalaf, David, author.
Title: Modern kinship : a Queer guide to Christian marriage / by David and Constantino Khalaf.
Description: Louisville, KY : Westminster John Knox Press, 2018. | Identifiers: LCCN 2018036073 (print) | LCCN 2018053350 (ebook) | ISBN 9781611649116 () | ISBN 9780664264611 (pbk.)
Subjects: LCSH: Same-sex marriage--Religious aspects--Christianity. | Marriage--Religious aspects--Christianity. | Interpersonal relations--Religious aspects--Christianity.
Classification: LCC BT707.6 (ebook) | LCC BT707.6 .K43 2018 (print) | DDC 261.8/35848--dc23
LC record available at https://lccn.loc.gov/2018036073

♾ The paper used in this publication meets the minimum requirements of the American National Standard for Information Sciences—Permanence of Paper for Printed Library Materials, ANSI Z39.48-1992.

Most Westminster John Knox Press books are available at special quantity discounts when purchased in bulk by corporations, organizations, and special-interest groups. For more information, please e-mail SpecialSales@wjkbooks.com.

To the memory of Mamatita y Papaché, who taught
me that love and marriage can last a lifetime.
— Constantino

For my parents, Jim and Dyanne, and my sister, Tamara.
Thank you for being my family, my tribe, my people.
— David

CONTENTS

⎯⎯⎯⎯ ⟳⟲ ⎯⎯⎯⎯

FOREWORD

The world needs this book.

I'm pretty sure those were my exact words to David and Constantino when they first told me about this project many months ago. A faith-based book about modern relationships that speaks honestly about everything from sex to shame to spirituality and isn't plagued by gender stereotypes and heteronormative assumptions? We've needed that book for years! Then, when they told me they were coauthoring it, I smiled politely and said a quick prayer for this poor couple who thought they could write a book together without killing one another first.

Bless their hearts.

Thankfully, both the book and the marriage survived—and the world is richer for it. From the first paragraph to the last, *Modern Kinship* is an eyes-opened, tenderhearted, practical, and winsome tribute to love, in all its mystery and messiness, that leaves the reader both awed and equipped. With pastoral care and good humor (which no doubt got them through those unavoidable creative differences), David and Constantino serve as reliable guides through the unique challenges faced by queer people of faith who want to honor God and their neighbors in their romantic relationships. Where their own experiences may be limited, David and Constantino humbly yield the floor to others: a trans man dating a woman, a bisexual woman married to a man, an interracial and interfaith couple, even a boring straight lady like me. The result is a tapestry of stories and insights that, when you step back, reveal the very picture of holy kinship Saint Paul told us we should see: that of Christ's love for the church.

The world needs this book because these stories need to be told. Of the volumes that have been written on faith and family, few, if any, offer real-world advice to LGBTQ people about the ups and downs, obstacles and triumphs they may encounter as they date, build friendships, marry, sort through their baggage, and start families as queer followers of Jesus. As a result of bad theology and historic prejudice, many LGBTQ Christians have to work harder to find role models who have been at this for a while. David and Constantino offer their mentorship with generous vulnerability—we learn from both their successes and mistakes—and that is no small gift in a culture where our public lives are so carefully curated.

But it's not just queer Christians who need this book. It has become popular in certain circles to talk about "including" LGBTQ people in the church, welcoming their voices to the table and serving them better. This puts the privileged at the center. *Modern Kinship* is yet another reminder that inclusion and welcome are reciprocal, that straight allies like me have just as much to gain from the full fellowship of queer siblings in the faith as they do. Christ set the table long ago; it is he who does the inviting. The Spirit has always led from the margins. Indeed, some of the most grace-filled moments of my life have happened when LGBTQ Christians invited *me* to the table— by serving Communion, by inviting me into their homes, by liberating me from the idolatry of gender stereotypes and binaries, and, in this case, by teaching me how to be a better wife, mother, and follower of Jesus through the stories of those whose experiences both differ from and are familiar to my own.

Finally, the world needs this book because the marriage at its center is a sacrament, an outward sign of inward grace. It is a gift of God for the people of God. What makes a marriage sacramental isn't the degree to which its partners reflect gender stereotypes, or stick to a list of rules and roles, or reflect cultural norms and expectations, or even get it right all the time, but the degree to which the love of Christ is present in one of the most challenging and rewarding commitments two people will ever make to one another. Just as there is something about the bread and wine that reminds us of Jesus' humanity, there is something about the tension and longing of romantic love that reminds us of our desire for God and God's desire for us. There is something, too, about the way we forge sacred kinships with one another, sometimes in unlikely or unconventional ways, that reminds us of how the whole world has been "grafted in" to the family of God. These relationships give us just a glimpse into the great mystery of God's relentless, unfailing, deeply vulnerable, and yet utterly unstoppable love for God's creation.

Marriage is not an inherently holy institution. And it cannot magically be made so by the government, a priest, or a catered event. Rather, marriage is a relationship that is made holy when it reflects the life-giving, self-sacrificing love of Jesus. All relationships and vocations—marriage, friendship, singleness, parenthood, partnership, ministry, monastic vows, adoption, neighborhoods, families, churches—give us the opportunity to reflect the grace and peace of the kingdom of God, however clumsily, however imperfectly. Orthodox priest Alexander Schmemann explains the tradition of crowning a couple at an Orthodox wedding as the moment when "here is the beginning of a small kingdom which can be something like the true Kingdom."[1]

Here, in this book, is a picture of a small kingdom that is something like the true kingdom — or, as some theologians prefer, the true *kin*dom. By sharing their stories and those of others, David and Constantino have followed the example of Jesus, who gave himself "for the life of the world."

The world needs this book. I'm so glad it exists. May we receive the gift of it with joy.

Rachel Held Evans
Author of *Searching for Sunday* and *Inspired*

INTRODUCTION

WHAT IS MODERN KINSHIP?

On the evening of November 2, 2015, moments after David said yes to my proposal of marriage, he grabbed me by the shoulders and said, "Look at me. Look me in the eye. From now on, I will be your family. I will be yours, and you will no longer be alone. I never want to hear you say you're alone again. I'm your family." Then we held and kissed each other. And we cried.

For the first time in many years, I began to feel like I had kin. Kinship is a bond based on shared experience and a shared identity that distinguishes you and your people from the rest of the world. Kinship is the commonality and sense of belonging that Adam expressed when he called Eve "bone of my bones and flesh of my flesh." This phrase is used throughout the Bible to assert a closeness that goes beyond friendship. We see Laban embrace Jacob in Genesis 29:14, saying, "Surely you are my bone and my flesh!" The Israelites crowned David using the same words. Your kin are the people to whom you belong and who belong to you, the people with whom you share your greatest joys and who help you through your deepest troubles.

A person without kin is alone at a primal level—an aloneness God recognized in Genesis 2:18 as "not good." God gave us the gift of kinship as a cure for that aloneness, and typically it has taken the form of marriage and children. Your kin are the family into which you are born or adopted, and the family into which you marry.

A decade before meeting David, I experienced the breakdown of kinship so common between LGBTQ people and their parents. And having lost the kinship into which I was born, I looked to marriage as a new promise for that bond. As a gay Christian man, the first question I faced was whether God's declaration that it is not good for a person to be without kin applied to me—whether I was worthy of God's promised cure for aloneness. Through prayer and the reading of Scripture, I discerned that the answer is yes. There is no doubt in our hearts that God has a plan for the well-being of LGBTQ people that is compatible with the way he created us.

David's bond with his family of origin has always been strong. When he came out, his parents dug into relationship and sought to help him the best way they knew how. Unfortunately, what David thought he needed at the time was reparative therapy. He spent almost two decades in a combination of therapy and men's "healing" groups. The messages he received during that time left him emotionally stunted. His feelings were so repressed that even his relationship with his parents, as close as it was, became superficial. In order to grow, he needed to heed God's call to romantic relationship. He had to distinguish the voice of the Holy Spirit from the voice of mere humans who claimed to speak for God.

Over time, both of us separately heard that still, small voice from the Spirit say in no uncertain terms that God welcomed us to find a spouse—in the words of Genesis, a helper fit for us. We heard God say that he would bless our union in marriage to someone of the same sex.

We believe God wants the marriages of LGBTQ people, like all marriages, to bear his image. We believe a marriage in God's image is trinitarian; it brings two people together, with Christ at the center. Christian marriage, as we understand it, is a lifelong covenant reflecting the covenants the Lord has made with his people. It is through this covenanted union in the presence of God that a couple becomes a new unit of kinship. And for queer people who often lose that bond with the people who reared them, the promise of marriage—the hope of someday having kin again—becomes one of the most beautiful messages proclaimed by the gospel.

This is modern kinship. It is a bond as old as humanity, made available in modern times to people who have heretofore lived on the margins. In a world inching ever closer to God's kingdom—a world where "there is no longer Jew or Greek, there is no longer slave or free; there is no longer male and female" (Gal. 3:28)—modern kinship includes the marriages of LGBTQ couples. This book is a window into such marriages.

Our ministry to advocate for healthy relationships in the LGBTQ community began during our engagement, when we found that there were virtually no resources to help queer Christians navigate the waters of marriage, church, faith, and sexuality. We started a blog as a way of processing and examining our own experience, and, to our surprise, we soon found that we had become the role models for others that we hadn't had for ourselves.

Our writing has forced us to be transparent about our relationship—not only about the good times, but also about the challenges and conflicts that come with marriage. We're grateful for the opportunity to share and inspire. It has given our marriage a sense of mission and has encouraged us to be more outwardly focused. Our hope has always been that, by pushing against the boundaries of our comfort zones, marriage would make us better friends to our friends, better servants to our community, better emulators of Christ. Writing publicly and with a critical eye about our relationship has helped us keep those goals front and center.

It is important to acknowledge that the experiences and beliefs of LGBTQ couples are as diverse as the queer community itself. We could never speak for all of us. We write through the lens of our experience as gay men who believe marriage is a monogamous lifelong relationship that has been cemented through a public act of commitment. Some will challenge our beliefs or our ways of approaching relationship, and we welcome diverging opinions. Our story is *one* way of doing relationship.

In the following pages, we will share with you the stories of other members of the LGBTQ and Christian communities and their experiences with relationship and marriage. We speak with, among others, Austin Hartke, a thought leader in the trans Christian community who transitioned while dating his girlfriend; Gabriel Mudd and Geoff Bleeker Mudd, who traverse the challenges of a same-sex, interracial, interfaith marriage; and Rachel Held Evans, a progressive Christian writer and ally who believes LGBTQ relationships have a unique role in speaking to straight marriages, especially in the context of complementarianism and gender roles.

The queer Christian community is moving past apologetics, beyond having to justify our sexuality to the church or defend our faith to our secular LGBTQ friends. For so long our community has been focused on the issue of acceptance that we have, perhaps, become shortsighted about what lies beyond it. That is what we seek to explore in this book: lives and relationships as they break free from a history of hostility and emerge into an era of acceptance.

We seek to reaffirm some aspects of marriage and challenge others. We hope to touch upon the universal truths of contemporary relationship, regardless of faith tradition or sexual orientation. And we want more than anything for readers to understand that even if some of us aren't built for marriage, each of us is built for kinship. For too long, Christianity has been characterized by dividing lines marking who is in and who is out. As the continual revelation of God's character encourages us to draw the circle ever wider, we hope to see a day when the entire mass of humanity is on the inside of that line, bonded by a common kinship.

CHAPTER 1

⌘

LONG LINES FOR THE TUNNEL OF LOVE

Let's all pause for a moment and reflect upon how the roller coaster called dating is, on the whole, a nauseating ride. Most of us, gay or straight, wait for our turn to ride the Tunnel of Love, only to discover that the line isn't so straightforward: it zigzags through the amusement park that is our lives, past Missed Opportunity Land, through Bad First-Date Town, and disappearing into the Emotional Baggage Grotto for who knows how long. And even as some people inexplicably keep cutting in front of us, we continue to wait in line with no guarantee that we'll ever actually make it onto the ride.

That part of dating is universal, but there's something uniquely challenging about the LGBTQ Christian dating experience. There are factors that seem to make our line a little bit longer, that make the wait outside a little bit hotter. These challenges aren't insurmountable, but if we hope to make it to the Tunnel of Love, it's helpful to take an honest look at the path we have to navigate to get there.

The most glaring disadvantage for LGBTQ Christians who want a partner who shares their faith is the dating pool. Imagine a Venn diagram in which one massive circle is the Christian population, and another, much smaller circle includes the LGBTQ community. The sliver of overlap between the two is small enough to make the dating pool look like a dating puddle. This won't come as a surprise to many of you who have thrown your hat into the romance ring. No matter how many profiles you swipe through on Tinder, the reality is that it's slim pickings for queer Christians committed to finding someone who shares your faith.

Before we started dating, we both tried out dating apps for a while and found them to be more entertaining than actually productive in finding a suitable partner. Thankfully, we still have single friends to entertain us by sharing dating profile pictures of, say, men posing with their ventriloquist dolls or offering unsavory close-ups of body parts. As for genuinely suitable matches of people seeking committed relationships grounded in faith, there were maybe a few dozen matches in each of our respective metropolises—Los Angeles and New York—and we already knew most of them. Dating puddle, indeed.

But do we really need five thousand choices, or even five hundred? In his book *The Paradox of Choice*, Barry Schwartz explores the idea that too much choice has conditioned us to be "maximizers," people who seek out the very best option rather than a perfectly satisfactory one.[1] The result is that we become hypercritical consumers, always on the hunt for the next best thing and never content to make a decision. That might be a great way to shop for a TV, but not a romantic partner. The smaller dating pool of the LGBTQ Christian community harkens back to a time when folks lived in isolated towns and were perfectly content to choose from the four or five people of marrying age in their community. Perhaps limited choice has its benefits.

Another challenge unique to the LGBTQ experience is the coming-out process. What many people fail to understand is that coming out doesn't happen all at once. There is no gay correlation to a bar mitzvah or confirmation, in which you read the sacred texts of Oscar Wilde in front of friends and family and then receive a rainbow flag from Ellen DeGeneres, who drapes it about your shoulders as a disco band strikes up "I'm Coming Out." There isn't a public notice in the newspaper (although many people do make the announcement on Facebook). Coming out necessarily takes place in stages, over time, throughout someone's life.

The difficulty in dating is that many LGBTQ people find themselves at different stages of the coming-out process. Self-acceptance is a long journey for many LGBTQ people of any faith (or none), and it's difficult to navigate a relationship while one or both of you are still reconciling your sexuality. It's such a common problem among friends in our community that we've given it a name: the Self-Disclosure Discrepancy Theorem. The theorem states that the more disparate you are in the coming-out process, the more stressful your relationship will be. A couple in which one person is completely out and the other is completely closeted will necessarily face conflict in even the simplest acts, such as going out to eat in a public place.

When we first started dating, this was a source of stress in our relationship because I (David), having struggled through years of reparative therapy, was still coming out to some people in my life. I felt pressure (mostly self-imposed) to come out faster than I was comfortable, and Constantino was uncertain he wanted to invest his time and his heart in a man who might bolt at a moment's notice. It was an emotional tug-of-war that we managed to work out only with a lot of compromise and communication.

Being at different stages of self-disclosure doesn't doom a relationship. However, it's important to talk about it up front and also to have ongoing discussions about expectations for the future ("When will we go to church together as a couple?" and "When will you tell your parents about us, if at all?"). You might date someone more closeted than you and discover that the stress and limits it imposes upon the relationship aren't worth it. And if you're the one who is mostly or fully closeted, you may be better served working on integrating your sexual identity into your life before you choose to enter into a relationship.

Ultimately, what prevents many of us from even getting in line for the Tunnel of Love is our baggage. Emotional baggage isn't unique to gay Christians; virtually everyone experiences sexual brokenness or dysfunction in some form or another. But whereas most people come to dating carrying an emotional tote bag or a suitcase, many LGBTQ Christians come with the entire nine-piece Tumi set. Many of us carry a deep-seated shame because we have separated ourselves from our sexuality to the point where it is something foreign or despicable. A relationship won't heal these wounds; rather, it will intensify them if they aren't addressed.

Researcher Brené Brown writes in her book *Daring Greatly* that shame is so powerful it's often the single greatest barrier in preventing meaningful connection: "Studying connection was a simple idea, but before I knew it, I had been hijacked by my research participants who, when asked to talk about their most important relationships and experiences of connection, kept telling me about heartbreak, betrayal, and shame—the fear of not being worthy of real relationship."[2] (We'll talk more about shame in chapter 4.)

The shame I developed from years of reparative therapy still causes me at times to form walls and push Constantino away. The unworthiness Constantino feels from treatment by his parents still causes him to develop narratives about our marriage that aren't true. We carry these wounds into relationship, and it does no good for us to pretend they're not there.

When you finally nab a seat on the Tunnel of Love, make space for that baggage. Seek out counseling if you notice your baggage getting in the way of intimacy and vulnerability. Be aware of your sensitive spots, and be able to communicate when they're triggered. Otherwise, you'll be apt to hop off the ride when it has barely begun.

I dated very little before meeting Constantino, and never seriously. Dating was more like a rogue mission, performed with the secrecy of a covert military operation. I never told friends or family; in fact, I barely admitted it to myself. Whenever I met some guy I liked, it was much easier for me to think we weren't dating but just hanging out frequently. Alone. And making out.

My reservations about dating grew out of my sense that it was a rebellion against God, as my six years of reparative therapy had taught me. Even as I came to believe God would bless a same-sex relationship, dating still felt shameful. It meant that not only was I admitting to my attractions, but I was actively pursuing them.

Emotional baggage has always been my roadblock to relationship. Long before reparative therapy, I had developed the belief that feelings were weak and to show or feel them was something to be embarrassed about. So I threw my feelings into the basement of my heart, locked them inside, and left them alone to take up scrapbooking, or whatever feelings do when left unattended. It turns out that emotions don't pursue self-actualization or higher education on their own; rather, they warp and atrophy until they become something like Gollum in *The Lord of the Rings*.

Those covert operations weren't really dating; they were play-dating. I was seeing what it was like to pursue romance without allowing myself any emotional connection to the men I went out with. When I allowed myself to feel, the overwhelming emotion was shame. No matter how thick the chains I wrapped around the basement doors, shame would eventually wriggle through the cracks and I would cut off ties with the men. This cycle repeated for years.

Enter Constantino. We traded a few messages on OkCupid while he was living in New York and I was in Los Angeles. I flirted in the way that was safe to do when someone lives nearly three thousand miles away. Neither of us had any interest in long-distance romance. But then he decided to fly out to California for a social weekend organized by members of Q Christian Fellowship (formerly The Gay Christian Network). I decided to go too, and I agreed to pick him up at the airport to carpool to the event in Pismo Beach.

It wasn't love at first sight because love, along with all of my other feelings, was safely locked away below, beside the rusty garden tools and jarred peach preserves. But there was a connection. I felt instantly comfortable with him, so much so that throughout that weekend people thought we were dating. For me, the word that kept coming to mind when I thought of Constantino was *teammate*. I remember it clearly because it was such a strange word for someone I had just met and was not in the least bit romantic. But I realize now that what I needed then wasn't romance; it was someone who would be on my side, willing to sit with me patiently as I unpacked my emotional baggage.

Later that year, Constantino moved to Los Angeles for work, and the friendship we had started eventually blossomed into romance. It was not a smooth ride; our relationship sputtered forward in fits and starts like a rusty jalopy. Constantino brought some of his own baggage, but it was mine that kept causing us to stall. At times my religious reservations and emotional unavailability seemed as if they would doom us. I showed him my basement and pointed out the thickness of the chains and the heavy lock on the door. *It's useless*, I wanted to tell him. *Just be on your way.*

But he didn't run away. Nor did he try to wrench open the doors. Instead, he sat down and waited. He earned my trust by the way he listened to me — really listened, without just waiting for his turn to speak. He inspired me with the way he tended to other hurting gay Christians in our area and formed a safe space for them to explore faith. And he attracted me with his infectious smile and romantic notions of what a good relationship could do and how it could serve not only the two people in it, but the community around it.

With time, my basement doors would creak open, and a feeling would peek its head out. Constantino would see it, engage it, and honor it for what it was. And when it ran back inside he didn't go chasing it down. He'd just sit and wait some more. Sometimes he'd pace, and occasionally he'd look between the cracks of the doors and call into the basement, getting at my emotions when I least expected it. He has made me cry before with just a gentle stare.

Now that we're a few years into marriage, my emotions more often live upstairs in the readily present parts of my heart. But the basement is still there, and when they feel threatened they go scurrying back to the dark recesses with which they're most familiar. Marriage doesn't heal your wounds (in fact, intimate relationship can often trigger them). There are days and even weeks when the basement snaps shut, when the feelings hide and regret having ever come out into the light. But next to the doors, I keep a chair just for Constantino. It's comfy and worn from years of use. Given enough time, the doors will reopen. It's there we reconcile. It's there I love him all over again.

God's a Wingman, Not a Matchmatcher

While not everyone suffers the same emotional unavailability, nearly all LGBTQ Christians have at some point struggled with integrating their faith with their sexuality, especially in the context of dating. We've heard many stories of women and men who, when they enter the dating arena, shed their faith like a jacket at coat check because it no longer seems to fit. As one of our blog readers put it, "My concept of God hasn't grown to encompass my new beliefs about sexuality. I decided to start dating and let my belief systems follow when they're ready. As a result,

I can't seem to make myself pray, or even generate much interest in God as a concept."

What does it look like to invite God into the mess of dating? Those of us from evangelical backgrounds probably shudder at notions of purity rings, accountability partners, and prayer groups. Gay and straight alike, the church has poisoned our concept of what it looks like to incorporate God into the dating process. We have been taught that we must be washed and waiting, standing like virgin wallflowers at a school dance until God pulls us onto the floor and allows us to dance (stiff-armed) with someone he (always "he" in that context) has chosen for us.

God as divine matchmaker is not a model that has worked well for many straight couples, and there's no reason to think the LGBTQ community will fare any better. What if, instead, we thought of Jesus more like our wingman? A wingman is not a matchmaker—his job is not to find the right guy or girl for you. A wingman's job is simply to help you navigate the dating field, holding you back when you're about to step on a mine, keeping distractions away when you decide to make a move, and buying you a drink when the attempt falls flat. He's there to revel in your successes and commiserate in your failures.

It's not easy. When we have spent our entire lives hearing that same-sex relationships elicit divine wrath, asking God to be a part of the process sounds like madness. An important first step for many LGBTQ Christians is to reframe God not as an antagonist, but as an ally. That requires getting to know God again.

If we want to invite the Spirit into the dating process, we may first need to meet the real Jesus for the first time, free of the filters our churches put upon him. Our God is not a distant, angry deity, but someone who personally knows human angst. God is that "hangry" guy who yells at trees when he's having a bad day, and who ugly-cries at the sight of his dead friend (even when he's about to bring him back to life). Jesus, fully human, must have longed for romance at some point in his life. Too often we think of Jesus' suffering only in the context of his death on the cross rather than the lifetime of ups and downs that formed his human experience. The Bible gives us but a window at Jesus' thirty-three years on earth, but even then, the picture that emerges is not of a stoic demigod who looks down on human beings. What we find is a man who is well acquainted with the full spectrum of human emotion. We see him overwhelmed, seeking solitude to get away from the crowds, and later lonely, feeling abandoned and forsaken in the garden. If we forget these daily sufferings, it becomes harder for us to believe that Jesus could ever know us and want good things for us.

Both of us invited Jesus into our dating process in different ways. Constantino came to the faith later in life, after having been out as gay for more than a decade. He attended affirming Episcopal churches in New York and felt confident that God would be OK with him falling in love and being with a man. However, his track record showed that he simply wasn't very good at picking them. Having grown wary of his own judgment, he prayed that God would point out those who wouldn't make a good match so that no time and effort would be wasted on them. He also confessed his loneliness and desire for relationship, not only asking God to help alleviate his solitude but to sit with him in it. For Constantino, Jesus was a wingman who commiserated.

On the other hand, I (David) grew up in a more conservative Christian environment and became active in evangelical churches as a young adult. Whereas Constantino didn't trust his judgment, I didn't trust my path and still struggled with uncertainty about what God and people in my life would think. I summoned my courage to start dating Constantino, but at the same time I prayed daily that I would feel convicted if the relationship was counter to God's plan for me. I didn't sit on the sidelines waiting for God's permission but tried to take careful, thoughtful action and seek God out for feedback. For me, Jesus was a wingman who gave advice and guidance.

Inviting God into your dating life is not a way to improve your chances of finding a partner, as if God were just a genie who grants wishes. Instead, it's a way to better integrate your faith into your life—into every messy, broken part of yourself. Turning our wounded parts toward God, especially in the context of sexuality, helps us see that God is not the one who has done the wounding. Rather, God is the one who seeks to heal our wounds.

There are no guaranteed success stories when it comes to dating. Some folks will wait patiently in line for the Tunnel of Love and never board the ride. It's not divine punishment, and quite often it's not a reflection of who you are. A lot of dating comes down to the right timing and circumstances. Which is to say, there's a fair amount of luck involved.

There are ways in which you can prepare yourself better for relationship (say, coming out or addressing your emotional baggage), but no amount of self-work will change the small dating pool we were talking about. No matter how sexually integrated and emotionally healthy you are, there's little hope if you pull up OkCupid (or Tinder, or Grindr for that matter) and find yourself staring at a screen that presents no viable options. To appreciate the awesomeness that is you, someone needs to see it from nearby.

Challenging Geographic Limits

This is the hard truth: if you're a single LGBTQ Christian who would like to be in a relationship with someone who shares your faith, chances are you'll have to move. As with every rule, there are exceptions. But if you're pinning your hopes on being the outlier, you're increasing the difficulty of a battle that is sufficiently uphill already.

In our social circles, this reality holds true. There are our friends who dated long-distance until one moved from Houston to Seattle (they're married now). There are other friends who tried dating while living hundreds of miles apart in Colorado but ultimately decided to both move to a new city out of state in order to live near each other. And we have a single friend who moved out of Charlotte because, after years of attempting to date there, he felt as if the culture and size of the city weren't going to yield the kind of partner he hoped for. We could go on and on.

There are already few enough fish in the sea; limit your search to your local pond, and you may never get a nibble.

"But only *one* of us has to move," you may say. "I just need to find someone who wants to move to where I live." True but problematic. Relationship requires a great deal of risk and a great deal of effort. If you're already heaping all of the risk on the other person while you're only willing to dish up the reward, you're starting off on the wrong foot. The possibility of you moving must be on the table. Even the most reticent-to-move guy we knew, a dyed-in-the-wool Manhattanite, eventually compromised and relocated to *Brooklyn* to accommodate his boyfriend — who moved from Washington, DC.

Our relationship is no exception. When we met, I was living in Los Angeles and Constantino was in New York. I loved aspects of New York (the energy, the subways, the halal carts), but I'd never want to live there (the crowds, the cost of living, the god-awful smell of . . . *what is that?*). Constantino had visited Los Angeles and had fun, but he had his own aversion to the city (the sprawl, the jammed freeways, the unrelenting sun). We were quite happy in our separate worlds.

Then we met, and suddenly our cities lost a bit of their luster. Neither of us was willing to date cross-country, so it seemed that our brief in-person encounter would end there. When Constantino got a job opportunity in Los Angeles through his work, he took a risk. I was the impetus for the move, but not the only reason. Constantino moved because he became convinced that, as much as he loved New York, he wasn't going to find the kind of relationship he was seeking in that city's frenzied dating environment.

Constantino took all of the risk upon himself initially, but the story doesn't end there. Even as our relationship flourished, something in Constantino's psyche shriveled. As much as he was growing to love me, he did not love Los Angeles. We decided for the health of our relationship to look for a third, neutral city that met both of our living needs. We wanted a place we could explore together, a new home where we could establish community and traditions as a couple. And so I left the comfort of Southern California, a place I had lived my entire life, for the sake of our relationship.

It may be that other considerations make it impossible for you to move. You may decide that in the end, what you'd be giving up would be too high a price to pay for a relationship. That's fair. Moving is also no guarantee that you'll meet the person of your dreams and fall in love. But if being in a relationship is something you prioritize, perhaps it's time to step out of your geographical comfort zone and start racking up those airline miles.

The move I (Constantino) made for David was no small decision. After growing up in Guatemala, a country in which I never really felt at peace, New York became the first place I felt at home. Although Spanish is my first language, I could never roll my Rs as a child. I still can't. What this means is that I have an accent both in Spanish and in English. I don't sound like a native anywhere.

New York, however, is a cacophony of accents and languages. No one gives you a second look no matter how you talk. It was in this city of immigrants and transplants that I felt most American and felt accepted as such.

I still remember what I posted on Facebook after returning from the weekend in California when I met David: "I'm back, NY. I love you. We need to talk." Carpooling up to the social event and then camping out in tents next to each other, we spent a lot of time together in just a few days. It felt comfortable; it was easy. I drove on the way back to

Los Angeles, and I remember thinking, "Why is this guy who met me four days ago letting me drive his car?" And that's when I started praying. I asked God, sincerely, that he guard me from falling in love with someone thousands of miles away. This prayer was denied in no subtle manner. I'll never forget the song that came on the radio as I prayed: a cover of Pete Townshend's "Let My Love Open the Door."

I went back to New York knowing, somehow, that I would have to leave the home I loved. Three months later a job in Los Angeles opened up with my company. I took it. I denied and will continue to deny that I moved across the country for a guy. That's just not the sort of thing I do. But as hard as it was for me to leave New York, heading west felt like the right decision.

David and I started dating three months after I moved to Los Angeles, and it was probably the rockiest time of our relationship thus far. David was still coming to terms with his sexuality, pushing me away even as he wanted to grow closer. I was stuck in a city that felt distinctly not my own, clinging to a person who felt ill-equipped for the intimacy I needed. I stuck around because he kept taking steps that surprised me.

Thanksgiving arrived only a couple weeks after we started dating. David wasn't prepared yet to tell his family about us or invite me to their celebration, but he didn't want me to be alone. So he held a "Friendsgiving" brunch before driving to Orange County for the family dinner. It was our first holiday together, yet it wasn't really together. I was encouraged, but everything still felt so tenuous.

Shortly after Thanksgiving he emailed his extended family to tell them he was gay. He shared the email with me. It was pure David—humorous yet sincere, feelings with a veneer of comedy. It made me fall in love just a little bit more. It made the promise I'd made him (that I'd wait for him to figure this all out) a little more honest.

I don't understand couples who are always 100 percent sure, who always have it all together, who are truly, madly, deeply in love—with cartoon hearts and butterflies peppering their every word. I'm suspicious of them. The job that took me to Los Angeles didn't work out, and I went through some rough times. This forced David and me to talk about our finances and spending habits early on. Sharing that aspect of your life with someone is like getting naked—in the least sexy way possible (more on that in chapter 11). But we discovered we could be on the same page regarding those matters and continue to work as a team. His mindfulness made me trust him.

I've spent a lot of time looking at him. It sounds creepy, I know, but I have. I love watching him work. I smile watching him talk, tell jokes, and pray. For us, the Tunnel of Love started out like a roller coaster, full of ups and downs. I'm sure there are loop the loops in our future, but neither of us regrets the ride.

Questions for Reflection

1. What do you see as the challenges of having a small dating pool? What opportunities might there be?
2. Our Self-Disclosure Discrepancy Theorem holds that the more disparate you are in the coming-out process, the more stressful your relationship will be. What experiences have you had with this? Were you the more closeted one or the open one, and how did that affect your relationship?
3. Do you agree that LGBTQ Christians are often saddled with more baggage than others? What kind of baggage do you bring to a relationship?
4. Did you feel as if you had to shed your faith when you began to date? How have you been able to reincorporate it?
5. Have you moved for the sake of a relationship or enacted some other major life change? What was the experience like? If not, would you consider it?

CHAPTER 2

―――――― ∽⟳∼ ――――――

THE JOURNEY THROUGH UNCERTAINTY

Theological uncertainty is one of the most common refrains we hear from LGBTQ Christians. They ask: How can I ever be sure same-sex relationships are OK? How can I know, unambiguously and unreservedly, that God would bless my relationship? That inner conflict doesn't end magically at the wedding.

We have a friend who got married not long after we did; she and her wife are both lovely, wonderful women. But our friend, who grew up as a pastor's kid in an Evangelical Free church, still grapples with worries about the biblical soundness of her marriage.

"Here I am today, knowing that my father's interpretation — the one I carried with me until just a few years ago — is off-base and just not the full picture, yet I haven't really adopted a new filter yet," she wrote in an online support group we moderate. "I'm literally afraid to pick up the Bible because I'm afraid of what I'll read. Everything I read I am ingesting through that old, disproved filter and

I am unable to shake the guilt and shame that bubbles up as a result."

Today's conservative church fails in the realm of uncertainty. In other words, the church idolizes certainty. It's no wonder why the advice many church folk give LGBTQ Christians is all law and no grace:

"What the Bible says about homosexuality is clear."
"Anything that could lead to sin is not worth the risk."
"The only safe path is celibacy."

These are easy declarations when it's not your own life on the line. It's much easier to tell someone else to stay inside with the doors locked and the curtains drawn rather than to go on a journey that involves risk. We have been raised to embrace safety and certainty.

We call this type of Christianity "answer worship." It's a kind of spirituality that relies so heavily on the need for certainty that believers refuse to move until they have an unequivocal message from God. What they fail to see is that uncertainty is not a weakness but rather a core characteristic of healthy faith.

Catholic priest and ecumenical teacher Richard Rohr describes uncertainty like this: "People of deep faith develop a high tolerance for ambiguity, and come to recognize that it is only the small self that needs certitude or perfect order all the time. The Godself is perfectly at home in the River of Mystery."[1]

Understanding uncertainty in this way transforms it from something that is fearful to something that is freeing. Once we understand that God will never fully satisfy our questions about same-sex relationship (as well as many other issues, for that matter), we can stop pursuing our quest for answers. We can let go of our need to know. Rather than quizzing us about our knowledge of the rules, God invites us into relationship. Bring your confusion and your anger and your grief over your uncertainty. All of that is welcome. God doesn't want us to seek answers; God wants us to seek the divine. *God* is the answer.

For those who insist on staying put until all of their answers are satisfied, we offer this: What if inaction based on fear of sin is more sinful than acting with a genuine intention to follow God? Perhaps it's better to misstep with the intention of following God than to never take a step at all. How can God ever use us if we refuse to crawl out of our self-imposed cages? How can we offer anything to others when all of our energy is focused on withholding and obeying? Ultimately, we can never truly know God's mind with absolute certainty.

Knowledge comes in many forms. A healthy faith is shaped not only by the Bible but also by our direct relationship with the Spirit and our lived experience. It's not the Bible that called the United States and other nations away from the practice of slavery; the Bible was in fact frequently used as evidence to support the practice.[2] Instead, an evolving consciousness shaped by the Spirit and personal experience showed us how wrong it was. The Bible itself features stories of people who had faith without knowing a thing about Judeo-Christian religious texts (the story of the Roman centurion in Matthew and Luke, for example). So as for the notion that the Bible is the *only* way to know and understand God, we couldn't disagree more.

One of our blog readers calls believers who embrace uncertainty the "sticky-fingered, messy-faced children" of God. We love this image of children exploring and engaging the world, who discover truth experientially even though they sometimes get into trouble or make a mess. So many of us have been taught to be the child in the corner, playing only with the toys explicitly designated for us and never venturing beyond our playpen for fear of breaking rules.

If we step out in faith, seeking the way to God in the dark wilderness of life, God will guide us to the wild adventures intended for us. If our hearts continue to bend toward the

Divine, God will correct us when we're off course, and will find a way to draw us back to the right path. The paradox is that the more we embrace uncertainty—the more sticky-fingered and messy-faced we're willing to be—the closer we may get to those answers we've been quietly waiting for.

Repairing What Isn't Broken

I (David) was neither sticky-fingered nor messy-faced growing up. My value was derived from the approval and affirmation of peers and authority figures, so I became adept at following rules, avoiding mistakes, and overachieving in all possible instances (see "Teacher's Pet," Foothill High School yearbook, 1996).

When I chose to come out to my family during my freshman year of college, the experience cracked my veneer of perfection, the one that for years I had polished to a shine like a middle-aged man with a new Porsche. Coming out felt like the ultimate breaking of rules. My sexuality felt like the worst of mistakes.

In my memory, the story of my coming out to my parents is always intimately tied to my first car—a bright red 1994 Dodge Neon. It was in that car that I sat in my parents' driveway for the better part of an hour, trying to gather the courage to go inside and have The Talk. I was nineteen, a freshman in college, and life was only just beginning; yet somehow this felt like the end.

After what seemed like forever, I did go inside, and I did have the talk with my parents and sister. And it did feel like the end. The conversation broke my family. Something had died, and it wasn't until years later that I realized it was something that had to die. It was the illusion that we were a perfect family, the facade that we had no deep problems. We sat and cried for a long time.

My parents told me they loved me no matter what, which is so much more than many LGBTQ children hear.

But they were also afraid and ashamed, and my being gay just didn't seem like an option for them. And so they found me a therapist—a reparative therapist. I went to him on and off for six years, racking up enough airline miles on my parents' credit card that they could probably have taken a first-class tour of the world.

My therapist was Joseph Nicolosi, who was *the* person to go to for same-sex attractions. It was like going to Stephen Hawking for advice on theoretical physics, or Richard Simmons for Jazzercise classes. Nicolosi was one of the founders of NARTH, the National Association for Research and Therapy of Homosexuality, which was created in 1992 after the American Psychiatric Association had, according to NARTH, "totally stifled the scientific inquiry that would be necessary to stimulate such a discussion [on homosexuality]."[3]

That season in therapy was intricately tied to USC football games, final exams, and late nights working at the school newspaper. Therapy ran parallel to my collegiate life, a secret alternate reality to the persona of a confident young adult I was trying so hard to create. I would disappear from campus for a few hours each week to make the drive from downtown Los Angeles up to Encino. Nicolosi's dark, cozy office was located in a nondescript building a few blocks from the freeway. My first time there I asked Nicolosi if the office would stamp my parking receipt. "We validate feelings," he said, "not parking." He didn't lack humor.

The premise of reparative therapy is to identify and heal our deep emotional and psychological brokenness; we are fundamentally disconnected from our sexual identities, and if we can heal the shame we feel about that, our natural, opposite-sex attractions will naturally surface.

Our sessions typically involved me talking, or sitting there trying to identify a feeling, while he quietly listened, scribbling inscrutable observations on his notepad. Half of my attention went into trying to interpret his chicken scratch so I could discover just how messed up I was. He wore a uniform of his own design: baggy slacks with an ill-fitting dress shirt, and never a tie. He was in perpetual need of a haircut. When he spoke, it was forceful and confident. I don't remember him ever expressing doubt. Maybe that's why I followed him for so long.

The problem was that, after six years, reparative therapy had the effect of increasing my shame, not alleviating it. No matter how hard I tried to develop greater intimacy with my father and form healthy friendships with masculine men to coax out my "true" sexual identity, my attractions never subsided. That meant I was somehow irreparably broken. I carried the label "fundamentally flawed" in my heart for many years.

Even after I stopped therapy, I spent another ten years in men's "healing" groups, doing a lot of talking but not a lot of healing. For most of my twenties I lived in a kind of limbo with my sexuality, coming to understand that my feelings wouldn't change and feeling helpless about what to do about it. I began living a fragmented life: gay friends in one corner, church friends in another. I felt as if there was no way for me to integrate myself. I felt dis-integrated.

Even more troubling for me than the shame was the theological uncertainty of same-sex relationship. I had lived through so many years of professionals telling me I was emotionally dysfunctional and broken, far from God's intended nature, that I had internalized this message as immutable truth. My heart was trapped in a cage of law while God was on the outside, beckoning to me down a different path. There was no way I could get to God, not with all my doubts. The thing about living in a cage of law was that it both trapped and protected me. Opening the door would free me, but it would also expose me to a world lacking certainty. Even if I could somehow accept my sexuality, down what kind of slippery slope would that take me?

When I was in these healing groups, the members (including me) were some of the most miserable, inwardly focused people I have ever known. Our hands were clenching so hard to obedience that there was no way for them to grasp onto anything else God might have for us. A good friend dealing with same-sex attractions once said to me, "It takes all of my energy just to obey. God can't ask anything more of me; I have nothing left to give." That was a kind of "aha" moment for me. There was no fruit in our lives. Mere obedience was not cultivating joy and freedom. I knew then that the way I was living was not the answer. The door had opened, but my theological uncertainties and deep shame made it difficult to step out of my cage. I also knew that if I didn't step out, if I stayed behind those bars for the rest of my life, it was as good as death.

Heeding the Call to Adventure

To stay with what we know or move into the unknown — this is the fundamental struggle that begins the hero's journey. Popularized by comparative religion writer Joseph Campbell, the hero's journey describes a fundamental human experience of receiving an invitation into uncertainty. For LGBTQ Christians, the "unknown" may involve embracing our sexuality, acknowledging our gender identity, or stepping into relationship without having all of the answers worked out. It's not easy to heed the call into the wilderness; this struggle between safety and adventure is so primal it spans mythology across all cultures. "You must give up the life you planned in order to have the life that is waiting for you," Campbell said.[4] Accepting our identities as LGBTQ Christians is impossible without first sacrificing our old, constructed identities.

A popular book on screenwriting describes this fundamental crisis of identity as "Stasis = Death."[5] At the outset of every story, the protagonist encounters a dilemma: she can stay the same and die (metaphorically or physically), or she can embrace change and face unknown dangers, possibly even death (metaphorically or physically). It's a damned-if-you-do, damned-if-you-don't situation. Watch any movie and you'll see it's true. What if Luke had stayed on his home planet instead of following Obi-Wan? What if Marty hadn't hopped in the DeLorean? What if Katniss hadn't volunteered to take her sister's place in the Hunger Games? Had they clung to the status quo, each protagonist would have died in his or her own way (stormtroopers, Libyans, a broken spirit). Stasis = Death.

Moving forward is necessarily one of the most difficult tasks we will ever undertake. Regarding the journey, Campbell has been credited with saying, "The cave you fear to enter holds the treasure you seek."[6] That is to say, the very thing we are looking for lies down the path we most fear.

Like every LGBTQ person who has ever come out, we have heeded the call to adventure ourselves. Constantino grew up in Guatemala, where gay culture exists exclusively underground, hidden and shunned by the rest of society. He knew that wasn't the life he wanted to lead, wearing a public facade of heterosexuality while keeping a "roommate" at home who was secretly his partner. And so when an opportunity arose for him to move to the United States, he left his family and the lands where they have lived for centuries. It was not an easy decision; in order to gain U.S. citizenship, he knew he wouldn't be able to return home for many years. He was sacrificing his old life to embrace one that was new and unknown.

I was living a comfortable, relatively full life in Southern California. But a part of me was lonely and isolated, and my unresolved sexuality felt as if my soul had a schism. When Constantino entered the scene, I had to make a choice: finally embrace and affirm my sexuality, or reject the opportunity and accept a life in which I felt perpetually unreconciled in my heart. I felt God opening the door to romance, but on the other side of that door was a long, dark cave. I had to be willing to travel the darkness to get to the treasure—Constantino—on the other side.

The mythology of the hero's journey is evident throughout the Bible: Abraham leaves a wealthy, comfortable existence for the promised land. Peter and the apostles abandon the safety of their community and travel the surrounding territories. Saul/Paul sheds his old identity and travels to the ends of the earth. There are no guarantees of happily ever after when we heed the call. Stasis leads to certain death, but change offers its own dangers and sacrifices.

Coming out is a hero's journey all its own. So is taking the step toward dating. Many of us hear the call to adventure but are held back by fears we have internalized from family or church. *How can I explain my need to them? How can I make them understand?* Unfortunately, you can't and you won't. It's impossible to explain your journey to others, especially when the "death" we face is nothing obvious but rather a feeling reverberating deep inside us. For Christians, the best response we find for moments like these is "I feel God calling me." As true as that is, it may be an unsatisfactory answer for family members who lament a journey they disagree with or don't understand. But the call is individual, and private, and personal; it offers no explanations, reasons, or justifications to others. This is why it takes a bold heart to respond.

When the Call Comes Late

Younger readers of this book may feel less intimidated by the journey. The tide of public opinion has shifted swiftly, and it's easier today to come out and be in a same-sex relationship. The church lags far behind in its acceptance, and those of us enmeshed in conservative communities, regardless of our age, will necessarily journey a path peppered with tough conversations with family and friends. But readers our age and older may feel as if they're too far down the road of life to embark upon the journey to relationship.

Our generation grew up during the purity movement and the heyday of Pat Robertson and Jerry Falwell. We lived as adults before marriage equality. We remember the AIDS epidemic of the 1980s and the stigma the disease carried. Being gay was not an identity to admit to; it was a secret shame that others saw as tantamount to a death sentence.

What might have seemed like a glimmer of light during the sexual revolution of the 1960s quickly turned to dusk. Countless gay, bi, and trans people of every gender suffered through those dark times—disenfranchised, exploited, and abused by a culture that devalued them. We honor the queer saints and champions who stood up and fought during those desolate decades. Many of them were not Christian, but they were setting the groundwork for the rest of us to understand God's love in more radical ways.

It was during that long night that many of us lost hope. Whether or not we were old enough to name our sexuality or gender identity for what it was, we knew there was something inside of us that could never be expressed. We felt as if there were something broken inside of us that we could never share. If we could take the famous words of Allen Ginsberg's poem "Howl" but update them to better suit this lost generation, they would be this: *We saw the best hearts of our generation destroyed by hopelessness, starving hysterical naked, dragging themselves through the straight streets at dusk looking for an angry God.*

Eventually dawn broke, and morning came. The legalization of same-sex marriage in Massachusetts in 2004 seemed at first like a strange anomaly. Then, in hardly more than a decade, Americans across the land began to change their minds, and marriage equality became federal law in the United States in 2015. It was a cultural change so swift it left many of us with our heads spinning. Even though we emerged into a new world more ready to accept us, the scars of our upbringing have made it difficult for many of us to accept ourselves.

As our sleepy eyes have adjusted to this new dawn, those of us on the verge of middle age or well into it may wonder if there is still time. Suddenly, that path we thought we had passed by years ago is standing in front of us. The weeds and the brambles have been cleared away; the journey is there for the taking. But many of us resigned ourselves to the well-trodden road so long ago that a course correction this late in life may seem impossible. The barnacles that have grown over our hearts don't slough off just because the tide of public opinion has turned.

What about those who "obeyed God" and married people of the opposite sex? They played by the rules we were given, and now the rules have changed. The uncertainty of hope is harder on them than the rest of us. We have many friends in this position, and they struggle with what their paths forward look like. Some choose to divorce and begin the search for a partner of the same sex. Others remain married—sometimes for the sake of their children, and sometimes because they simply can't imagine life without their spouse. No matter what they choose, the decision feels gut wrenching, and it is not one most of them want to make unilaterally. A friend of ours who's in a mixed-orientation marriage wrote an anonymous guest post for our blog admitting that the angst he feels is not his alone—it is shared by his wife.

"For years, I played the victim," he wrote. "I bemoaned the fact that I was walking through this life without intimacy, healthy sexual fulfillment, or that deep companionship that everyone longs for in a committed relationship. And then one day, it hit me: My wife is walking through life in exactly the same way." Our friend, who has chosen for now to remain married, ended the post on a wistful note: "Despite all of the pain and agony of being in a mixed-orientation marriage, it is often within the beauty of the tiniest things that I see God. I see him in the beauty of nature and I see him in the gifts that we give and receive. And, to be perfectly honest, I hope someday I get to experience what it feels like to get the gift of flowers from a man."[7]

Regardless of our age, almost every LGBTQ person has what many call a "second adolescence." During our teens, when our heterosexual peers are beginning to date and fumble their way through attraction and romance, most of us are only at the beginning stages of figuring out and reconciling our sexuality. It may be years before we come out and begin the dating process. So while many of our straight friends may be in committed relationships, married, or even married with children, we're only just figuring out the joys and tragedies of romance: learning how to ask someone out, experiencing rejection for the first time, and feeling the rush of budding romance. We're still teenagers at heart even though our bodies are twenty-five, thirty, thirty-five, or older.

Because so many of us enter the dating game at a later age, it's common to have a nagging sense that we had better find "the one" soon. We're summer chickens trying hard to make it feel like spring. But the call to adventure doesn't work on our timeline; just ask the Bible's Sarah, who laughed at God's idea that she would bear a child in her old age. Even so, the hero's journey is for everyone, not just the young. No matter your age, there is hope. We may not be children anymore, but we can still be sticky-fingered and messy-faced if we choose to be.

Questions for Reflection

1. Do you need certainty before you can fully embrace your sexuality? If so, how has that worked for you?
2. What would a faith full of ambiguity look like? How would it make you feel?
3. Have you endured reparative or ex-gay therapy? How did that experience shape your sexuality? How has it impacted your faith?

4. Have you ever experienced a "hero's journey," when you felt compelled to embark on an adventure even if others couldn't understand why? What was that like for you? Would you consider coming out a hero's journey?
5. Have you ever felt "behind" in the dating process compared to your heterosexual peers? What is that experience like? Have you felt a need to catch up or to make up for lost time?
6. What advice would you give to gay people who married spouses of the opposite sex because they thought they were obeying God?

———————— ∞∞ ————————

DATING AS A
TRANS MAN

The hero's journey of Austen Hartke had a few more twists and turns than most. When Austen met his girlfriend of five years, he was still presenting as a woman. His girlfriend had never dated someone of the same gender before, so falling in love with Austen meant she had to go through the process of coming out as gay. Then, about a year and half later, Austen came out as transgender. "It was kind of a funny thing," Austen says. "We had to do the whole thing all over again, and be like, 'Actually, never mind, now we look straight.'"

Dating and navigating the nuances of being in a relationship presents different challenges for transgender people than it does for cisgender gay men and lesbians. "I think there are two sorts of stereotypes about dating trans folks," Austen says. "Either you are so complicated and messy that you're not worth dealing with, or you're the best of both worlds. As a trans guy, I've had both of those things leveraged at me."

The first thing many people fail to understand, in Christian circles especially, is that gender identity is independent from sexual orientation. The LGBTQ experience is not a spectrum—trans people are not "gayer" gay people. The LGBTQ acronym simply refers to a community of individuals who experience gender and sexual or romantic attraction differently from the majority of the population.

A cisgender person is someone whose internal sense of gender matches that which society identified for them at birth (most likely based on their anatomy). This is the experience of the majority—including the majority of gay people. But what we have learned in recent decades is that there is more to gender—our own sense of being male, female, or perhaps neither—than what is signaled by our body. People whose gender doesn't match the anatomy with which they were born are called transgender. And just like cisgender people, trans folks can be sexually attracted to members of the same sex, members of the opposite sex, or both. In other words, they can be gay, straight, or bi.

Austen identifies as bisexual, and he first came out as such when he was in his teens. He is now twenty-nine. He has been in long-term relationships before, but his current girlfriend is the only person he has dated since his transition. She was supportive from the beginning, wanting him to feel comfortable in his own skin. "I'm really lucky that she was that wonderful," he says. "It was nerve-racking for me. She was the first person that I talked to deeply about what I was feeling, and about my gender, so to open up to someone and talk about that felt really vulnerable and really emotional. But every single time, she was very supportive and asked, 'Tell me more; what can I do to better understand and to support you?'"

That kind of reaction to a person's transition from their significant other can feel like a lifeline, but it's not necessarily the norm. Among transgender men, says Austen, it is common that coming out and transitioning results in a loss of community—especially if they've presented as women and identified as lesbians for a long time. "For women who identify as lesbians," he explains, "it feels like you're in a marginalized group because you're a woman, and on top of that you're in another marginalized group because you're gay. This gives you a very strong sense of community, and of taking care of each other—watching out for each other. So when you transition and start being read as male and identifying as male, it's a hard thing to figure out. On the one hand, this is your family, but on the other, as a male you don't want to get in the way of the female spaces that your friends who are lesbian need as part of a marginalized community."

That complicates things when it comes to dating. A straight trans man who previously dated lesbians might find that the women in his old dating pool are no longer interested in him. A gay trans man may discover that cisgender gay men are reticent about dating a guy whose body is different from theirs. Austen says this makes it hard for trans people to find spaces where they can safely seek a partner: "For trans folks, dating apps are not as inviting and welcoming a space most of the time because we tend to get those people who are either like, 'You're gross,' or like, 'Oh cool, now I can fetishize you.'"

Austen walked through the process of coming out and then transitioning alongside his girlfriend, but for other trans people, the question of when to tell a potential partner that they are trans can be a matter of life and death—especially for trans women, says Austen, because they are at a higher risk of being physically hurt or killed when they come out. "The process of disclosure has to be individual not just to the trans person who is coming out," he explains, "but also individual to the person that they are telling, because you have to be able to trust that person, essentially, with your life." As for himself, he has never been what people call "stealth," meaning someone who tries to pass for cisgender. "I've always been very upfront about it, partially because I don't want the fact that I'm trans to come as a surprise to anyone, because that's the main reason trans folks get killed." Often, murderers of transgender people will try to use the "trans panic defense," claiming that they were so surprised that they didn't have control over their actions. "I understand the people who do want to go stealth," says Austen, "because if they don't, they have to deal with all the anti-trans stuff. But that is why the process of disclosing when you're trans is such a touchy one, just because of safety."

Austen, who has a master's degree in Old Testament from Luther Seminary in St. Paul, Minnesota, wrote a book called *Transforming: The Bible and the Lives of Transgender Christians*, in which he discusses the unique challenges faced by transgender people of faith as they seek to integrate into church communities. Diving deeper into his faith has led him to embrace marriage as a good thing and as something he wants for his life.

"When I was younger," he explains, "I never thought I was going to get married, because my parents got divorced. My thinking was that marriage is something that ends anyway, so what's the point of getting involved with it in the first place?" As he's gotten older, however, he has begun to understand how important family is to him, and he recognizes that the best way that we as humans have figured out to create a family unit is through establishing covenants.

"The one thing I have really latched onto has come through faith and my study of the attributes of God and the Bible," he says. "One of the basic attributes of God is fidelity and faithfulness—to the people of Israel, or to the church—and we have a call as Christians to be people who keep our covenants, and that's something that I really value. With that, my view of marriage has gone from something that was very negative to something that is very positive."

He and his girlfriend have now begun discussing the possibility of getting married and what that life might look like for them.

Austen's relationship advice:

"Whenever you recognize change starting in yourself—whatever that may be—share those feelings about change with your partner while you're going through it. Don't wait until you think you have it figured out and then present the solution to them. Instead, let them walk with you on whatever journey you are on."

CHAPTER 3

―――――――― ∽∾ ――――――――

COMPLICATIONS IN
COUPLING

So you're dating. You've embarked on that journey of adventure; you've hopped on that ride and you're entering the Tunnel of Love. Huzzah! Now you and your partner simply coast along the breezy, leisurely ride to happily ever after, right? *Right?* (Insert awkward silence.)

As is the case with the married friend we mentioned in chapter 2—the one whose father is a fundamentalist pastor and who finds it dangerous, still, to read the Bible—relationship doesn't cure our lingering baggage and theological uncertainties. Quite often it serves to rouse them from their slumber and send them pacing up and down the hallways of our minds. Even if we think we've worked through our fears and issues, we often find that putting relationship into practice is a whole different beast.

David once wrote on our blog about the hang-ups he had while we were dating, and a straight, married reader commented: "Are you embarrassed/ashamed of being gay? If not (hopefully), why the reticence? . . . If you're afraid that people won't like you because you're gay, do you really want to hang out with them?"

He was trying to be helpful, but the comment amounted to a polite version of "Get over it!" Heterosexual allies take note: "Straight-splaining" an LGBTQ person's experience is not an empathetic approach.

This lack of understanding highlights a fundamental difference in the experience of dating between straight and LGBTQ Christians. Heterosexual Christians, unless they're violating some other dating taboo, never question the acceptability of their relationship. They might doubt a specific partner, but not the act of partnering. Despite the lack of biblical evidence, most contemporary Christians frame dating and marriage as fundamentally good and preferable to singleness. In fact, today's evangelical church is so obsessed with the traditional family unit that marriage has become a God-ordained destination to wholeness. It makes sense why someone growing up in that paradigm would be unable to empathize with a gay person's experience of dating.

The LGBTQ Christian, however, typically questions the process every step of the way. Dating often erupts in fits and starts, like an old car engine sputtering to life. It may feel unnatural at first because it is unpracticed. Imagine that all of us were taught to waltz at a young age but a few of us—the gay ones—never really took to the dance. We either gave up the activity or tried to mimic everyone else with our wooden moves. Later in life, we learn about a dance called the salsa, and we immediately fall in love with it. But the moves are new and, although it's still a form of dance, the energy of it is wholly different from the waltz we grew up with. It's necessarily going to feel both exhilarating and awkward at first.

Similarly, those in a same-sex relationship for the first time may feel awkward using the terms *boyfriend* or *girlfriend*. Those words are strange enough if you're dating later in life, but they become particularly heavy on your tongue if you've never used them before. That's why some people opt for the term *partner* or devise some other term that seems to suit the relationship better.

When we first started dating, David had trouble with the word *boyfriend*. Although he had been out of the closet for a number of years, he was still in the bedroom, crouched behind a chaise lounge. He had practiced a kind of don't-ask, don't-tell policy about his sexuality, and so only the closest circle of friends knew he was gay. Using the word *boyfriend* in conversations with other people was emotionally taxing because, in almost every instance, he was coming out to someone. Casual chat felt suddenly invasive, because even the most superficial question could prompt an admission that felt intimate and personal.

By dating openly, we give up control of who we come out to and when. For those who have fully reconciled their sexuality, that's not an issue. But for those who have withheld this personal information in areas of their lives — say, at work or with a more conservative group of friends — dating may force a lot of conversations you wouldn't have otherwise had. Partnering up for the first time can be as stressful as it is exhilarating.

Although it took some adjustment, we came to love the words *boyfriend* and now *husband*. They're shorthand ways of telling someone you're gay without having to actually say the words. In casual conversation it's sometimes difficult to come out to people directly; this poses a challenge for those of us who want to be fully known. The more we come to embrace and value our sexuality, the more we want to let people in. Being able to throw out the word *boyfriend* is an easy way to insert vulnerability into a conversation.

Women don't have quite the same luxury with *girlfriend*, since the word can also refer to a platonic friend. And since physical affection between women is more socially acceptable, it may be easier to hold hands or embrace in public without raising an eyebrow. That may be a relief for a woman who isn't ready to be fully out, but it compromises the visibility of lesbian couples and misses an opportunity to normalize these relationships in the public eye.

Many in the LGBTQ community may say that it's not our job to normalize same-sex romance and that our relationships shouldn't be an educational experience for others. There's truth in that, and we've certainly felt exhausted ourselves sometimes from dispelling misconceptions about gay love. However, we also understand that many people, especially straight Christians, won't take a step toward understanding LGBTQ romance unless someone in their lives is willing to illuminate the path. If no same-sex couple is willing to be a bridge to explaining LGBTQ relationships, then people will fall back on the misconceptions and stereotypes they know.

Rejecting and Embracing Dating Stereotypes

One of the great misconceptions of gay male couples is the "gay twin boyfriends" phenomenon. It's when two guys who look a lot like each other decide to date. They dress alike, get similar haircuts, grow matching beards, and look *oh so cute!* It feeds into a generalization that gay men only care about banalities like fashion and looking adorable — as if we were life-size Ken dolls done up to delight straight women. But even more consequential is the age-old criticism that gay men are extreme narcissists, so in love with ourselves that we want to be with someone exactly like us.

If you've ever met me (Constantino) in person, chances are you've seen me wearing my favorite style of shoes: slip-on Chuck Taylors. They're comfortable and, in Portland's casual culture, they work in most social occasions. I've gone through many pairs. I love Chucks. The problem is, so does David. And at some point before we met, we both bought identical blue slip-on pairs. I remember wearing mine the day he and I were introduced as new members at our church, back when we were still dating, before we lived together — before we could say things like "I put them on first—*you* go change!" So guess what he wore that day? *His* blue slip-on Chucks. Add to that the fact that we both had on polo shirts and shorts. I was mortified.

The similarities between David's and my style don't end there. We both wear newsboy hats a lot. We wear jeans and plaid a lot. And we sometimes (OK, often) wear the kind of form-fitting shirts that a friend's sassy eight-year-old daughter once declared "too small!" So we often end up dressed alike. It used to happen a lot when we were dating due to the aforementioned inability to see what the other was wearing before going out. And what did we always get? "You two look so cute!"

It used to make me cringe. I can handle tough conversations about theology and serious questions about sexual orientation, and I've always been able to shrug off an insult or two. But I couldn't stand being called a cute couple. I had to ask myself why it bothered me so much. Why did I even care? I realized it was because that matchy-matchy cuteness fulfilled the "twinsies" stereotype about gay male couples.

In the evangelical world, where so much is made of gender complementarity, this "twinsies" stereotype has ramifications. I've never bought into the notion that certain roles in marriage ought to be established based on gender. I think that stems from a simplistic and wrong reading of Scripture. But during our season of dating and engagement, I was very aware of the fact that there are people who would question the sanctity of my marriage to David because of our sameness. The last thing I wanted was to give them fodder.

David and I were substantially more sensitive to appearances when we were dating than we are now. Years of marriage and membership in a truly Christlike church have helped us care less about the opinions of people who don't know us. But both then and now, there are many assumptions people make when they first meet us, and our stubborn personalities used to hate it when we proved those assumptions right.

We have made many decisions throughout our relationship that are not what people would expect. For example, when we first started meeting people in Portland, most were surprised to learn we didn't live together. People are surprised now to hear we sleep in separate beds—which has nothing to do with prudishness and everything to do with the fact that we just don't like playing tug-of-war with blankets and sheets. And when the conversation gets deeper, people are still surprised to learn that we didn't have sex until we were married.

We have made these decisions out of personal preferences and ethics, not out of any sort of legalistic adherence to Scripture or out of a desire to circumvent stereotypes. Many of our friends have made wildly different choices in regard to dating and marriage, and we believe there is space for a wide range of approaches to relationships as long as couples are having conversations and developing their own thoughtful ethics (see chapter 4 for more on sexual ethics).

The "gay lifestyle" is not monolithic. So then, to what extent do gay Christian couples have a responsibility to dispel stereotypes? Many would say we have none, and they could make a strong case. But with so much misunderstanding and rumormongering in certain corners of the church, I believe that we should seek to provide a variety of examples of what being gay looks like. Not at the cost of our uniqueness, but because of it.

Were either David or I to stop wearing the kind of shirts we each like or the shoes that make us feel comfortable just to intentionally look different, it would be false to who we are as individuals. One of us would be losing his personality. So we've resigned ourselves to sometimes matching, to sometimes being "gay twin husbands" in muscle shirts.

Same-sex couples can impact their churches by simply being themselves. They shouldn't embrace the customs and mores of mainstream gay culture if that's not who they are. Conversely, they shouldn't suppress behavior that others may construe as a stereotype just to conform to expectations.

If you're a "twinsie" couple, embrace it. Chances are you've already spent a long time trying to be someone you're not just to please the church. It's time now for you to live out your own faith and to live by the ethics that God — not those who claim to speak for God — has moved you to accept. That's my goal for David and me. We're both now in leadership at our church, and if our shoes match when we stand in front of the congregation, so be it.

Affection as Activism

Displaying the diversity of same-sex relationships is one way we can help others better understand the LGBTQ community. Another is being more bold in the way we show affection in public spaces. We've had many dinner conversations about visibility and the role public displays of affection play in normalizing LGBTQ romance for a broader audience. Television has played a significant role in this. We were old enough to witness TV's first gay kiss in 1991 between two female lawyers on *L.A. Law*.[1] The scene was more spectacle than social progress; it prompted a spate of "lesbian kiss episodes" that were inserted for shock value and ratings rather than character development or plot advancement. We both vividly remember what was supposed to be TV's first gay male kiss on a 1994 episode of *Melrose Place*. The scene was heavily marketed, but the kiss never actually took place. Fox deemed the act too controversial, and so just as the two men leaned in for a slo-mo smooch, the camera cut away to a reaction shot of another character who witnessed the act. (It would be another six years before an actual male-male kiss was shown on an episode of *Dawson's Creek*.)[2] Regardless of where people stand on the issue of same-sex marriage, few would dispute that higher visibility of same-sex affection helps to normalize these relationships.

The two of us are not particularly touchy-feely in public. At our wedding, guests witnessed little more than a quick peck between us when we were pronounced kin. Scroll through the photos of our honeymoon, and you'll see us standing shoulder to shoulder on a beach in Croatia, sitting side by side on the ledge of a ruin in Montenegro, leaning over opposite sides of a table in Istanbul. We might just look like two "bros" on a buddy backpacking trip. When we kissed at midnight at a New Year's Eve party nearly two years into our marriage, a friend commented that it was one of the first times he had seen us do so—and he was at our wedding!

Although we're very affectionate with each other, it's something we typically reserve for our private moments. We've wondered whether we should be more affectionate in public as a way to normalize same-sex relationships for people in our lives who still aren't comfortable seeing it. There's a gap for some people between knowing a person is gay and seeing actual evidence of the fact. To know that a coworker or neighbor is gay may be tolerable, but to see that same person express affection for a partner may elicit discomfort. It's not only LGBTQ opponents who are challenged by physical contact; there are many people who want to be allies to the queer community (parents and family, for example) who still suffer aversion at seeing same-sex public displays of affection. We'd be remiss if we didn't mention that even some gay people themselves are uneasy with seeing same-sex affection.

Why does public affection matter? Orlando gunman Omar Mateen, who killed 49 people and wounded 58 others in a mass shooting at the Pulse gay nightclub in 2016, reportedly once stated that he got "very angry" at seeing two men kissing each other in front of his wife and child.[3] Although we may never know Mateen's true motive, people often hate what is foreign or strange to them. Those who are uncomfortable living in ambiguity revert to dualistic thinking in which everyone like them is good and everyone who is different is bad. This mindset is a toxic kernel that sprouts into arguments, fights, holocausts, and wars.

Historically, gay bars and clubs have been "safe spaces" because they are places in which members of the LGBTQ community can touch and kiss without drawing stares or negative attention. Although it is far safer and easier these days to be affectionate in public, each year still sees headlines of same-sex couples who have been assaulted for touching or kissing in public. LGBTQ couples are still enough of an anomaly in faith communities that they draw attention: a covert stare during worship, or perhaps a more explicit comment after the service. Depending on your church, some of this attention may be quite positive and welcoming; in other cases, it carries the full brunt of religious hostility. Either way, it can be difficult to date without the feeling of *being watched*.

When LGBTQ couples intentionally avoid public affection, it perpetuates a cycle. Simple acts of affection may be one critical step in normalizing same-sex relationships. For a while, we had challenged ourselves to be more affectionate in public, but we quickly realized that it's not our style; it's inauthentic to who we are. So we touch when it feels right and try to neither restrict nor fake our public displays of affection. Our hope, however, is that couples who want to be affectionate will feel increasingly safe doing so. We'd like to see a future in which no one bats an eye when a man at church puts an arm around his boyfriend, or when a woman gives her wife a loving peck on the cheek. The normalization of affection in public spaces will dispel fear-based intolerance, and rather than obsessing over how people touch each other, we can instead focus on the humanity of the people we're staring at.

An Uninvited Spotlight

In church communities, it isn't only physical affection that draws attention to same-sex couples—it's the mere fact of being. Because gay dating is still relatively rare in many

Christian denominations, individual couples often become for people the de facto models of same-sex relationship. Gay marriages are to some a stranger beast yet, and so these couples can become for a congregation the paradigm of how same-sex union works.

A married gay couple with whom we're friends endured a long and invasive process to become members of the Mennonite church they used to attend. There were special meetings and extensive discussions. The two were required to stand before the congregation and answer personal questions about their relationship. They were interviewed, poked at, and prodded in a way no heterosexual couple ever is. And although they were ultimately admitted as members to this church, the process soured them on belonging to that community.

In churches where there is no consensus on the sanctity of same-sex unions, a couple might feel as if it is up to them alone to prove their love is God-honoring. At more affirming churches, the couple might feel like a token, and their relationships with other members of the community might feel superficial. Either way, these are unfair positions to be in, and they place added pressure to relationships that already face more than their share of stressors.

We were reminded of this when two of our friends, who got married only about a year before us, announced their divorce. They are both kind, faithful men, and although we don't know the reasons for their separation, we can only imagine how difficult and painful the decision was. While we root for all marriages, we find ourselves especially invested in same-sex marriages, in part because we are all too familiar with the external challenges the partners have overcome to get to the point of marriage. Same-sex couples have jumped many hurdles just to get to the starting line; it feels particularly disappointing when those marriages fail.

Whether LGBTQ couples are dating or married, many eyes are on them in church, and we imagine the same is true when they break up. We were still dating when we first started attending our current church, and as far as we knew, we were the only regularly attending same-sex couple. We had a sense during those early months of being seen only as *the* gay couple—in no small part because our church expanded its marriage practice to include same-sex couples shortly after we started attending, and it was a point of fierce contention. The decision had nothing to do with us, and most of the attention we received was positive, but it nonetheless created stress about what the success or failure of our relationship might mean for people still shaping their views on homosexuality. *What if we failed? What would people think about us? Would it affect people's beliefs about the goodness of same-sex marriage?*

We're committed to the health of our marriage first and foremost because we take seriously the vows we made at our wedding. But we also acknowledge an existential fear that failure would somehow damage the case for other same-sex couples. We recognize this is mostly an unfounded worry, but the fact remains that there are many Christians watching and rooting for the failure of same-sex relationships. For example, one of our friend's parents, after learning their son had been dumped by his boyfriend, celebrated the breakup. They told him the split was heavenly intervention and was evidence of how much God despised gay sin. How dreadful to be told the failure of your relationship is divine judgment! This kind of attitude is evidence that, invited or not, the spotlight on same-sex relationships exists, and it makes some of us feel responsible to represent the queer Christian community well.

The LGBTQ community is one in a long list of outliers who have sought acceptance from the mainstream. That list includes women, foreigners, racial minorities, the diseased and disabled, and the poor and homeless. The further we are from whatever is conventional, the more likely we are to draw attention. And if we are one of only a few examples, as is the case with gay couples at church, people will look to us as representative of the group we embody, no matter how diverse that group is. There is a danger in taking on this yoke, however; feeling responsible for representing our community to the Christian world can stifle the authenticity so many of us long for in our faith communities. If gay couples try too hard to put their best feet forward for the sake of those watching, then we're only perpetuating the superficial, "#blessed" facade that has plagued contemporary Christianity. Just like heterosexual couples, gay couples fight, make mistakes, and sometimes break up. It's OK if people see the full range of our experiences.

Until same-sex relationships become more normalized in faith communities, they will always draw a degree of scrutiny. That's why it is so important to have greater visibility of LGBTQ couples in the church. Our hope for the future is that when LGBTQ Christians date, they won't be *the* gay couple at church—they'll be *a* gay couple. Better yet, they'll just be *a couple*. We are fortunate in that our social and faith communities are now more diverse than ever. There are many other same-sex couples at our church, including women, older couples, and ones with children. We are now less distinctive, which diffuses the spotlight. We fit into our communities more seamlessly because we're less unique—and we wouldn't want it any other way.

Dating doesn't make you a spokesperson for the LGBTQ Christian community, and yet it does. Coupling up creates greater visibility, and with that may necessarily come more attention and more questions from members of the church. Whether couples choose to engage or reject that responsibility is up to them. After all, the dating experience is your adventure; it's your journey into the Tunnel of Love, and it's your prerogative to decide to what degree you'll share the ride with the outside world.

Questions for Reflection

1. Have you ever questioned the validity of your relationship? How has that impacted the relationship?
2. Have you ever had to defend your relationship? If so, from whom? Has that stressed your relationship, or made it stronger?
3. Have you felt awkward using dating terms such as *boyfriend* or *girlfriend*? Are there other terms you use for the person you're dating?
4. What is your experience of showing public displays of affection? Does it come easy to you, or is it a challenge? Why?
5. If you're coupled, do you ever feel as if others are observing you as a model of LGBTQ relationship? What is that experience like?

CHAPTER 4

⎯⎯⎯⎯⎯⎯ ⟡⟡ ⎯⎯⎯⎯⎯⎯

SEX, SHAME, AND
SPIRITUALITY

In the Mailbag section of our blog, in which we answer questions from readers, most submissions are related to sex: *Do you feel guilty having sex? Does physical intimacy deepen your love for each other and God? Has marriage cured the shame you feel around sex? Can you get cancer from gay sex? How does gay sex even work?*

Although some of these questions are thoughtful, many of them give the impression that the LGBTQ population missed sex education entirely—which, in a way, we did. Even those of us who learned in school about the mechanics of sex between a man and a woman never learned what would one day be relevant to us. The result has been a vast swath of the LGBTQ population that has been educated about sex through the internet, pornography, and other informal means.

Whereas school failed to give us a complete education, the church poisoned our understanding of sex through a campaign of miseducation. LGBTQ Christians aren't alone in this. A straight Christian friend of ours once joked that

James Dobson, founder of Focus on the Family, ruined a generation of young Christians on sex. He wasn't wrong. Dobson and his organization, which espouses many conservative ideals, is particularly obsessed with issues related to sex and marriage: promoting abstinence, denouncing pornography, upholding gender roles, and rallying against LGBTQ rights.

Many of us, gay and straight, grew up in the purity culture movement, replete with chastity rings, modesty standards, accountability groups, and, yes, even daddy-daughter purity balls. (There were no mommy-son purity balls—*thank God!*—which only serves to highlight the inherent iniquity between the value placed on a young woman's virginity and a young man's.) The point of these programs was to manage, mitigate, and minimize sex. But sex is not a chronic disease; it is a beautiful expression of our humanity—a metaphor, even, for the work of the mutually self-giving Trinity we know as God. Dobson and those like him would have better luck parting the sea than controlling the sexual urges of teenagers.

The conservative church's solution to sex has been a three-pronged attack: ignore, suppress, and distract. It ignores the issue of sex as if the elephant in the room were not stomping about, knocking over lamps and chewing on the furniture. Many of our friends who come from homes more religious than ours grew up utterly ignorant about sex. No one ever gave them "the talk." One straight friend's father only offered to tell him about sex as he and his wife were about to leave their wedding reception to spend their first night as a married couple—too little, and much too late. If and when the church reluctantly recognizes sex, its solution for young adults is to suppress it: to chain the elephant up, starve it, and hope it withers away before it breaks any of the fine china. Young adults who can't tear their eyes away from the starved, chained beast are then distracted with Bible verses, prayer circles, and visualizations of the "reward" of a future spouse, when the beast can finally be unchained.

As twisted as that model is, there is at least a kind of logic in it for straight Christians: they are promised an idyllic union blessed by God. LGBTQ Christians, however, are never promised a future spouse or the joys of building a family. If God doesn't change their sexual feelings and ignite a (safe, controllable) desire for the opposite sex, they are ushered into the next room, that of celibacy. There is no elephant in that room, only white padded walls with no windows. The problem is that the church confuses the elephant for *sin* when really it's just *sex*. Sex is not a transgression against God but rather a divine desire built deeply into the core of our beings. If we are forcibly separated from our sexuality, it's not the elephant that will wither and starve, but us. Celibacy in the Bible is always framed as a gift from God, not a sentence handed down by the church. We respect and honor those who feel moved to celibacy and choose it freely for themselves, but treating it as a lifelong solution to "aberrant" sexual desire is a flawed premise from the get-go.

Neither of us had ongoing exposure to the worst of the conservative evangelical movement, but I (David) once attended a Focus on the Family all-boys basketball camp when I was about twelve. It was free throws and ball skills by day, and fire and brimstone by night. Every evening, at the mandatory "concert," a speaker would illuminate for our group of prepubescent boys all the ways in which we were failing God.

One night, after a set of contemporary Christian pop, the speaker took the stage to inform us about the evil popular music we couldn't listen to. Top on his list was Paula Abdul's hit song "Opposites Attract." He took umbrage with one line: "I make the bed, while he steals the covers." The speaker said it implied that the two were having sex before marriage. Mind you, this was the same year that saw the release of Madonna's cross-burning "Like a Prayer" video, Tone Lōc's "Wild Thing," and 2 Live Crew's "Me So Horny." Conversely, Abdul's music video shows her dancing with an animated cat, à la Ginger Rogers and Fred Astaire.

Even then, I recognized the absurdity of the church's nitpicky preoccupation with sex. (I may also have been personally affronted, since the first album I ever bought was Abdul's *Forever Your Girl*.) The church was effectively saying that all popular music was off-limits. Even seemingly harmless songs could subtly warp our fragile minds and have us stumbling headlong into sex. And having sex was, in no uncertain terms, the Worst Thing Possible. At a time when I was just learning to love music, the thought of having to abandon it for God was painful. That was the first experience I had in starving the elephant in the room, and it would foreshadow the rules and asceticism imposed by my reparative therapy years later.

The church will argue that these rules are training wheels to keep us from falling down. The problem is that these training wheels never come off, at least not until marriage, and by then we may not be able to function without them. Christians raised in this rule-based culture never really develop a sexual ethic of their own; they obediently adopt what the church has told them and are never allowed to question. This is especially true for LGBTQ Christians who trusted the church's instruction to marry members of the opposite sex—all with the promise that marriage would transform their desires. When that failed to happen, and ex-gay ministries began to crumble, the church adopted a celibacy-only policy. If God didn't change the desires of LGBTQ Christians, it was a clear call to lifelong abstinence. This is where the Roman Catholic Church and most Protestant denominations worldwide stand today.

A Theological Wolf in Sheep's Clothing

You cannot build a healthy sexual ethic on "Don't do it."
Queer Christians have never been given a framework for a
God-honoring sexuality, and the result is that sexual desire
often builds pressure and then erupts in unhealthy ways.
The uncomfortable truth is that many gay Christians who
can't reconcile their faith and sexual orientation often slip
into promiscuity as they navigate conflicting expectations
and desires.

I (Constantino) once briefly dated a man who was smart,
attractive, and Christian. He had grown up in the church
and was well versed in theology. Like many gay people who
grow up in the church, he'd been on a roller coaster as he
came to terms with being gay. He'd gone from having something called "accountability software" on his computer that
reported his online activity to his pastor, to dancing for tips
in a Speedo at a bar in West Hollywood. By the time I met
him, he'd gone back to school, gotten his master's degree,
and was cautiously returning to the church.

We were sexually active when we started dating, but
a few weeks in the guy suggested that we stop; he said it
didn't feel God-honoring and that he wanted to wait until
marriage. Shortly thereafter, he dumped me and shifted
gears again, jumping on hook-up apps and seeking out
casual sex with strangers. I puzzled over someone who
claimed to want a monogamous, faith-based relationship
but then quickly changed directions.

One explanation stems from a warped theology instilled
in some Christians regarding sin and repentance. The idea
is that we are all sinners who can't escape our weaknesses;
we all fall to temptation from time to time, but we've been
saved, so all is forgiven as long as we repent. In this view, it
is only open rebellion—being unrepentant—that is unfor-
givable and what dooms us to hell. If we combine that
idea with the doctrine that all same-sex relationships are

sinful, we end up with a theology that finds promiscuity preferable to monogamy. Committing to someone of the same sex would mean committing to a life of unrepentant sin, whereas the "trip up" involved in casual encounters is an offense from which we can easily seek forgiveness. Straight Christians will relate to what is arguably the most pernicious effect of this theology: it drives many to unsafe sex practices, because buying condoms, using birth control, or taking PrEP pills to prevent HIV transmission is seen as premeditated sin. Conversely, something that "just happens" is an accident for which grace is more easily received.

Christians who adopt this view of God—a boarding-school matron rigidly policing their sex lives—feel like it is better to meet up for anonymous, secret sex, to have multiple partners, and even to indulge in whole seasons of debauchery and lust as long as they ultimately repent. It is a familiar cycle for many gay Christians, and the biggest problem with it is the guilt and shame that compounds in their hearts over weeks, months, and years.

In addition to the dangers inherent to risky sex, this cycle drives people away from God. Scripture and human experience reveal that celibacy is a gift reserved only for some. If you are straight, try to imagine being told you must permanently abstain from sex (not only until you're married, but for life), while in your heart you don't feel called to celibacy. Imagine spending years praying that God will either change your sexual orientation or numb your desires for intimacy. Imagine trying one therapy after another, often at severe emotional and financial costs. Imagine praying for just one thing, but the one thing you ask for is the one thing God continuously denies.

This is the story of most LGBTQ Christians. It's not surprising, then, that so many queer people say to God, "I've done everything I could to give up this need. If you won't help me, if I'm on my own, I give up. I can't change my nature, but I can reject you as you have rejected me."

This is the tragedy of a forced-celibacy doctrine. We can't think of a better example of a wolf in sheep's clothing than a theology that, in its practical application, favors reckless promiscuity over commitment. Jesus' words in Matthew 7:17–18 come to mind: "In the same way, every good tree bears good fruit, but the bad tree bears bad fruit. A good tree cannot bear bad fruit, nor can a bad tree bear good fruit."

Exalting Queer Bodies, Discerning Sexual Ethics

We all lose when we blindly allow the church to determine our sexual ethics. As we discussed in chapter 2, one of the great tragedies of contemporary Christianity is its obsession with "answer worship." By claiming foolishly to know all the answers about sexuality and the ways to mitigate sexual sin, church leaders leave no space for members of their congregations to seek answers on their own. Self-guided discovery is a powerful way to draw closer to God; it removes the middleman, who is always too eager to interpret and filter conversations between us and God.

Both of us have spent many years developing our own sexual ethics informed by the Bible, our personal relationships with God, and our lived experience. Our ethics have not bent at every cultural whim, but they have been transformed over time as we've come to know God better. Even as our beliefs around expressions of sex have changed, our core sexual ethics have remained constant—which is to say, we fundamentally believe sex is good, a gift from God used to express a unique and particular kind of intimacy between human beings.

One of the core ethics we shared when we first started dating was that we wanted to wait to have sex until we got married. It wasn't because we thought ourselves purer-than-thou, and it wasn't because we think sex is dirty or bad. We don't care for legalism, and we don't think premarital sex is sinful. We chose to wait because we have come to believe sex plays an important part in establishing a bond of kinship between two people, and we believe that bond is sealed with the covenant of marriage.

Sex is a form of communication. We use it to say things such as "I love you" and "You're hot." Sometimes it's to say, "I'm sorry," or even "I'm lonely." Sexual abusers use it to say, "I have power over you." There are many things—good and bad—we can express through sex. One of those messages is "I am uniquely yours, and you are uniquely mine." In other words, we can use sex to physically express the promise of the marriage covenant.

There are many ways we can tell each other how strong our love is. There are many ways in which we can say that we find the other person attractive or can tell the other person, "I'm sorry." But we can't think of any way other than sex in which to *physically* express the covenant of marriage. And that promise is so important to us that although neither of us was a virgin when we met, we no longer wanted to use sex to say anything else. We chose to wait because we didn't want to say with our bodies something we hadn't yet said with our lives.

Opinions on reserving sex for marriage vary wildly within the Christian community, queer or otherwise. Some have accused us of being prudes and of not being "sex positive." Neither of us feels particularly prudish, and we both enjoy sex so much that we feel quite positive about it! Furthermore, we would never say that waiting until marriage is a mandate for all. In fact, blind adherence to that belief can lead to premature decisions about marriage, simply because the couple is eager to have sex. Those who find that sex is their driving motivation for marriage are probably not ready for it—and delaying sex might not be what serves them best in the long run.

Instead, we want to invite queer Christians to seriously consider what sex means to them in the context of their faith. We exhort them to pray and seek the counsel of wise friends, and with that, to develop a sexual ethic that honors their dignity as children of God—an ethic that respects not only their own integrity but that of others. We have many Christian friends (gay and straight) who have carefully considered their sexual ethics and have ultimately decided not to wait until marriage. We appreciate the thoughtful approach they've taken. It's the ones burdened by unexamined legalism and crushed by shame who sadden our hearts the most. And although we don't blame them, we worry about those who—having been hurt and failed by the church—assume a licentious and cavalier attitude toward sex.

Sex cannot be treated as a mindless sport or a leisure activity that has no consequences on our soul. A casual approach to sex, and the anything-goes culture that has developed in mainstream queer circles, particularly the gay community, has not led to happiness and integration for most who've experienced it. Michael Hobbes has written in detail about what he calls "the epidemic of gay loneliness." He describes a toxic environment that leaves many gay men feeling isolated, even in the most progressive and gay-affirming cities. We have both experienced firsthand the isolation described in the article. "In our lifetime," writes Hobbes, "the gay community has made more progress on legal and social acceptance than any other demographic group in history. . . . Still, even as we celebrate the scale and speed of this change, the rates of depression, loneliness and substance abuse in the gay community remain stuck in the same place they've been for decades."[1]

Depression and social isolation happen in all groups. Straight people suffer their own share of grief, and lesbians have unique struggles being both gay and women. Trans people face pressures and stress that cis men and women will never fully comprehend. Hobbes, however, looked at the particularly severe social isolation among gay males: "In a survey of gay men who recently arrived in New York City, three-quarters suffered from anxiety or depression, abused drugs or alcohol or were having risky sex — or some combination of the three. Despite all the talk of our 'chosen families,' gay men have fewer close friends than straight people or gay women."

Hobbes goes on to quote a respondent in a survey of care providers at HIV clinics who said, "It's not a question of [gay men] not knowing how to save their lives. It's a question of them knowing if their lives are worth saving." Our hearts break when we contemplate the fact that gay men continue to suffer even in the most progressive and affirming circles. It hurts even more to admit that gay Christian men are just as isolated, just as lonely, and just as prone to self-doubt. We were all lovingly created by God to bear the image of the Divine. Our lives are worth saving. And to be perfectly clear, we are not talking about an abstract salvation of our souls. We are talking about our bodies. Our physical, incarnate, bodily lives are worth saving. Queer bodies are worth saving. And we mean *all* queer bodies, be they cis or trans; male, female, neither, or both; curvy, skinny, or muscular; black, brown, white, or any other shade of skin. Sexual ethics matter because we are all worthy of respect, honor, and celebration.

Western Christianity has misunderstood the gospel, paying lip service to the incarnation and sidestepping the significance of the bodily resurrection. We have been taught that salvation is only about the soul and that the flesh cannot be trusted. This theology has been a whip whose lashes have tortured queer bodies for centuries. We have been bloodied — many of us literally, having been led to cutting and self-harm — by sermons telling us that our yearnings are mere physical impulses that must be resisted for the sake of our spirit. Our bodies have been unrepentantly destroyed by queer bashers who feel justified by those sermons. Yet the risen Christ is proof that the body matters, and the body must be saved.

"Look at my hands and my feet," Jesus said to his disciples upon his resurrection. "See that it is I myself. Touch me and see; for a ghost does not have flesh and bones as you see that I have" (Luke 24:39). We are not ghosts or apparitions. Like God, we have flesh and bones—muscles, hair, and skin. Our soul resides in our body; God's self, the Holy Spirit, resides in our body. And this divine incarnation is the only reality we can ever know. Divorcing the body from the soul creates a dissonance in our psyche that leads only to disintegration, blinding us to the image of God in ourselves and others.

Sex matters because it is the closest two humans can get to each other, because the pleasure it brings is a reminder that life is worth living—that our bodies are worth celebrating. An unexamined and promiscuous approach to sex empties us and leads to loneliness for the same reasons that puritanical mores and forced celibacy do: they deny the reality of God's creation and the heart of what God sought to teach us by becoming human and resurrecting in the flesh.

Decoupling Shame and Sexuality

Many Christians, especially LGBTQ Christians, carry deep shame around sex and sexuality. How do we go about unwinding the tapes of bad theology? How do we move toward healthy relationship when we are chained in place by shame? There are no quick fixes.

Shame is a powerful emotion because it is embedded deeply in every culture to regulate social interactions. When we violate what is seen by the group as good, right, or proper, we experience shame. It's helpful to understand shame in this way because it serves a purpose: it serves to regulate society and keep it functioning smoothly. It is passive law enforcement. Shame is meant to deter actions that violate codes of community. Shame might also be understood as a feeling that arises when we do something that grieves God. It is shameful, for example, for parents to kick out their queer child because of something a pastor told them. And even sexual shame has a place: it is shameful for men to disrespect the dignity of women and act as if they can get away with sexual abuse.

In this way we can appreciate what shame is *meant* to do. The problem arises when shame is misplaced. Then, the outcomes are disastrous. Even though Western culture is now largely accepting of LGBTQ people, we may still experience shame for being gay because we live in a church community or in an area of the country in which being queer is a violation of social norms.

Shame is misplaced when the rules and values that are enforced by it are corrupt, unjust, or misguided. These values may say that a certain race of person is not welcome in a community. They may set strict boundaries over how women can act and engage. They may denigrate and disenfranchise lower classes in the community. Shame is like an invisible boundary around a community of people; as such, it's more likely to touch the outliers than the people in the middle. LGBTQ people are still very much the outliers in most communities.

LGBTQ Christians may come to relationship with two kinds of shame: violative and internalized. *Violative shame* stems from having violated one of a community's social taboos. This could be having sex with someone of the same gender, fostering a habitual relationship with pornography, or dressing and acting in a way contrary to gender norms. Some queer Christians come to a relationship carrying the compounded shame left by the cycles of promiscuity and repentance discussed earlier. They may feel shame about their past actions—scarred in a way that makes them feel unworthy of love or incapable of committing to one person.

Internalized shame tells us that we are flawed, broken, and irrevocably damaged. Many LGBTQ Christians adopt this belief as they grow up even if they don't receive explicit messages about their worth. Internalized shame has been especially damaging in ex-gay and reparative therapy circles, in which women and men who have tried hard to change but failed have come to the conclusion that something inside of them is too broken to ever be fixed. We have friends who suffer from post-traumatic stress disorder because of their experiences in trying to heal their sexuality.

Violative shame is easier to overcome because it is situational. It derives from actions we've committed, which we can point to and say, "That's not me anymore" or, "That cultural code is wrong." Internalized shame is much more nefarious because it points to a flaw in the core of our being. When LGBTQ Christians hear that they are fundamentally broken, perverse, and sinful people, this message gets written across their psyches like law etched on stone tablets.

How then do we start to wipe this message away when it seems so permanent? Some have asked whether marriage helps to heal this shame. Perhaps, having entered into a holy union blessed by God, the spouses would experience the Spirit's shattering of those messages that have haunted them all their lives. Some may indeed experience sudden freedom from shame, but in our experience and in the experience of those we know, it takes years to walk away from shame, and it only happens one step at a time.

Shame within sex is an ongoing struggle after marriage for many heterosexual people too. We hear women talk about it far more often, perhaps because they have better emotional intelligence, but most likely because the purity culture movement has done a better job of shaming them. Writer Lily Dunn captured the experience in an article for *Relevant*:

> No amount of intellectual knowledge could take those deeply ingrained feelings towards our sexuality and magically change them the moment we slipped on those rings, or later when we slipped off our wedding clothes. It isn't really strange that this transition didn't happen instantaneously, what was stranger was that we expected it to.[2]

Her account is not unusual. Search the internet and you'll find pages of testimonies of married Christian women struggling with sexual shame. All of which is to say, just because LGBTQ people feel shame within the context of dating or marriage doesn't mean the relationship is wrong or sinful; it means we are sending ourselves false messages. Misplaced shame is pernicious. It destroys relationships, and it cripples people from the inside out so that they become a shadow of the person God would have them be.

I (David) have a long and intimate relationship with shame. From the moment Constantino and I started dating, our relationship was a plunge into a deep-end study of shame: what prompts it, where it comes from, what it's truly about. I used a word with Constantino when something about being in a same-sex relationship made me uncomfortable: *icky*. Early in our relationship, pretty much everything was icky: holding hands, kissing, saying "I love you" in anything more than a half-mumbled murmur. I attribute my moments of revulsion to cultural norms that have perverted the concept of homosexuality and to years of reparative therapy that conditioned me to see any same-sex affection as fundamentally dysfunctional. The "ickiness" was a waxy residue I could never wash off myself. It was an invisible layer that prevented me from being fully present, authentic, and vulnerable in our relationship. Even at my closest moments with Constantino, the layer of ick separated us.

That waxy coating of ickiness began to wear off when I stopped trying to answer the question of how I came to be the way I am and instead began to trust that, whatever the origins of my attractions, God had a hand in making me this way. The more I've learned to listen to the Spirit and unwind the tapes I've had playing in my head for decades, the less power shame has had over me. But that change has happened over years, not over the one afternoon we exchanged vows. When I feel most aligned with the Spirit, and most in tune with Constantino, there is no space for shame. I feel free to express myself using the full spectrum of matrimonial communication (which is a fancy way of saying I don't feel shame when we have sex). At the same time, the Holy Spirit hasn't waved a magic wand over me and wiped away all feelings of shame. When I'm in a bad place, or living too much in my head, it's easy for shame to sneak in and speak false messages to me. The waxy layer of ick can always build up on me again.

Queer Christians of evangelical backgrounds who aspire to marriage but have reservations have asked if we feel "convicted by the Holy Spirit" because of our union. The answer to that is easy: no. During our season of dating, I prayed frequently and asked hard questions of the Spirit: *Am I twisting theology for my own selfish purposes? Am I fooling myself or other people? Am I refusing to see truth that others claim to see?* No, no, and no. None of those questions rang true in dating or in marriage. In fact, more and more we feel the Spirit's peace over us. When I have opened my heart and asked God to show me the path he would have for me, it is Constantino's face I have seen.

For many conservative Christians, a personal answer from the Holy Spirit will never be sufficient evidence that God blesses same-sex unions. We won't try to convince them. But underneath the shouts of law and dogma, we recognize the Spirit's soft, subtle voice. If it proclaims goodness, then we will embrace that truth, and live it, and forever let it flow through our beings.

Questions for Reflection

1. Would you say your sexual education was in some ways a miseducation? How so?
2. What message did the church give you about sex growing up? How have your beliefs about sex changed?
3. Do you believe sex is a form of communication? If so, what have you used sex to say? What do you want to use it to say?

4. Do you believe the body is as integral to our beings as the soul? Why or why not?
5. How has shame shaped your sexuality and attitudes toward sex?
6. Some people believe in waiting until marriage, and others don't. What sexual ethics have you developed for yourself, and how did you come to them?

An Interview with Emmy Kegler

─────────── ∞ ───────────

A QUEER WOMAN,
A PASTOR, AND A
SOON-TO-BE WIFE

Not all queer Christians grow up stunted by shame because of their sexuality. The Rev. Emmy Kegler was raised in an affirming family that attended an affirming Episcopal church. "The congregation had a women's group, as many congregations do," Emmy says, "and even in the late 1990s, they were including a trans woman in that group. I remember I turned around one Sunday when I was little, and I shook her hand. Afterward I said to my mom, 'Mom, that lady doesn't look like the other ladies.' And my mom said, 'That's because she was born a man, but now she's a lady.' So I was just like 'OK!' In hindsight, it all seems incredibly progressive, but at the time it was just the norm for me."

Emmy realized she was gay when she was in her midteens. Seeking a more emotional worship experience than the one afforded by her stoic Episcopal Church, she joined a youth group at an Assemblies of God megachurch. There she encountered resistance to being out, but her response was to leave rather than put up with shaming. She was confronted by the youth pastor when she refused to sit through a sermon about the evils of homosexuality, but her foundation was strong enough that it didn't shake her. "I really was very fortunate as a teenager," she says. "Encountering opposition when I started pursuing my call to ministry is another story, but as a teenager I didn't have a lot of scarring experiences, which I know in some ways makes me very unique, and I'm very grateful."

The stirring in Emmy's heart that told her God wanted her to be in ministry started at about the same time that she awakened to her sexuality. And it was that call that led to some of the heartache familiar to all LGBTQ Christians. It also complicated her love life. She knew it would be difficult to be an openly queer pastor, so she resisted the call at first. "I thought you could be gay and Christian, and even gay and a pastor, but I decided that it would just be too emotionally difficult," she says. She remembers the consecration of Bishop Gene Robinson, the first openly gay person to serve in that capacity in the Episcopal Church. He had been elected to serve the Diocese of New Hampshire, but his election had to be affirmed by the General Convention, which was meeting in Minneapolis. "I was there," Emmy says, "because I was back in the Episcopal Church at the time. He had to wear a bulletproof vest at his consecration, because there were enough credible threats against him for daring to be an ordained gay bishop. And that was definitely a moment for me of pausing and saying, 'I'm not sure I want to do this. I'm not sure I want to pursue a call to ministry.' So I tried not to."

However, the call was not easy to evade. Emmy attended a Lutheran college, and it became clear there that she was called to become a pastor. She loved attending daily chapel, and the classes that excited her the most were the ones about religion. Her immediate environment, again, was very affirming. But it was 2004, and at the time, there was no path to ordination in the Evangelical Lutheran Church in America for people in public same-gender relationships.

Policies eventually changed, so she went to seminary and became ordained.

While she was waiting for a permanent position at a church, Emmy met Michelle, who is now her fiancée. Before that, however, dating was a challenge. Emmy tried to go on dates and meet women online, but her profile stated clearly who she was and what she was planning to do with her life. "I was open not only about my Christian faith but about my call to ministry, and there is a whole subset of the queer female population for whom dating someone like me was just not an option. People are just not interested in getting involved with someone who's not only a Christian but a pastor! And that's a completely legitimate perspective, in my opinion, considering what the church has done."

The picture Emmy paints of trying to meet someone will be familiar to any LGBTQ Christian who has ever opened a dating app. Most of the time, the women she met online who weren't put off by her faith turned out to be deeply conflicted about their sexuality. "There was one person I met with whom I'd been messaging back and forth, and it seemed like things were going well," she says. "Then I found out that she went to a nonaffirming church. And she was like, 'Well, we just don't talk about it.' And I'm thinking, 'How can you not talk about the fact that your church thinks you're a sinner, and that if they knew this about you they would no longer let you be part of the community?' I validated her decision to not talk about it, but that would just never work for me."

Then came Michelle. They had exchanged messages off and on over the course of about six months before Michelle finally wrote one day and said she'd been raised Catholic and had been thinking a lot lately about the relationship between her sexuality and her faith. She casually mentioned that she'd love to meet sometime and talk about that. "I was immediately like, 'Great! Clear your schedule. Let's do this!'" Emmy says. They met up for margaritas, and what was supposed to be a short date before Emmy left for an evening worship service became an hours-long conversation until the venue closed.

They are now engaged, and we asked Emmy why, in an era when more and more couples are choosing to remain unmarried, they are choosing marriage. "The purpose of marriage as it is today—creating a two-person, monogamous unit, legally bound; creating a one-home, single-tax-paying structure in which to raise children—those are all things I want in my life," she says. "I want to have a partner that I share a house and finances with, a partner with whom I raise children, a partner who has promised to love me even when I inevitably screw up, and who wants to continue working things out as we grow and change."

Emmy wants to make those promises before God because although she admits to struggling with the concept of providence or divine fate, her relationship with Michelle has developed in such a way that the easiest way to explain it is to say there was some kind of divine hand involved. "I know too many people who've gotten sick or faced profound struggles in life for me to just say, 'Oh yeah, God has a plan,'" she says. "But we believe God had some kind of influence in bringing us together. Our lives have had such an impact on each other's spirituality and mental growth that for us, making the commitment of marriage before God and before a religious community has become very important."

Emmy's relationship advice:
"Learn to fight well, because even soul-mate relationships involve conflict. Even if something seems perfect for the first year, five years, ten years, people change. Life changes us. Your spouse should be someone you can fight with, whom you also want to fight for."

CHAPTER 5

꠸꠸

IN SEARCH OF SUPPORT

One of our greatest conflicts occurred before we were officially dating, when we were in what is supposedly the fun, easy season of courtship. I (Constantino) was still new to Los Angeles and was having trouble adjusting to a car-centric city, a job I wasn't enjoying, and the loneliness that comes with moving somewhere new. I had an emotional crisis in David's apartment one night and couldn't bring myself to return to the ugly little studio I had rented in an unsightly part of town. Although David tried to comfort me for quite some time, my refusal to leave had him feeling emotionally trapped. Once I finally left that night, David decided that would be the last time we would see each other. It very nearly was.

We both felt utterly alone in navigating our first big conflict. I had no community in Los Angeles. David had plenty of friends but was going to a church that was not affirming. There was no one with whom we felt safe talking through our issues. There was no community to give us advice or support. Counter to most couples' experiences, that season of early dating was one of the hardest in our relationship, in large part because we were doing it in isolation. Time apart and an honest talk allowed us to work through that conflict, but we still count it as a minor miracle that we navigated through that difficult season.

Marriages thrive in community. They wither in isolation. Every couple, gay or straight, needs external support. We need friends and mentors to encourage us and advise us when times get hard. We need them to cheer and celebrate with us when good things happen. And we need their company and love during those long stretches when nothing big is happening—when life becomes routine.

LGBTQ couples are far less likely to have that kind of support. Those who have anchored their identities and their social circles in the church may find themselves suddenly adrift when they begin to date someone of the same sex. They are left to navigate every aspect of relationship alone.

Compare that to what happens when a straight couple at church starts getting serious. The two are celebrated, encouraged, perhaps even prodded along. If they get engaged, it is almost assumed that they will get some kind of premarital counseling—in fact, many churches require it. When we got engaged, however, we didn't even consider seeking counseling. We wanted to learn how to communicate better, and we wanted to support each other's spiritual growth, but church didn't seem like the place to get counseling, and we weren't sure a secular couples' therapist would fully understand the nuances of our experience as a religious couple.

Our pastor, however, offered to counsel us in the months leading up to the wedding. His invitation came as a wonderful surprise. Like so many LGBTQ Christians, we were used to feeding on the crumbs of the church experience, but this felt like being offered a seat at the table. His invitation also reminded us how complacent we had become about being second-class citizens in the church. We didn't expect our relationship to be treated with the same respect and legitimacy as other couples. We had come to accept that being marginalized and unacknowledged was normal. Although we've never been treated with hostility, our experience had been that same-sex couples are, at best, politely ignored at church.

Herein lies a major problem with the conservative church's rejection of gay couples. It's not only an abstract theological position; it has significant consequences for the health of gay relationships. When churches withhold services to gay couples—including workshops on healthy dating, premarital counseling, and classes for new parents—they create real and lasting damage in these relationships. Church leaders claim that their refusal to offer support services is simply an extension of their beliefs on homosexuality, but the effect is far more nefarious. By withholding relationship services from gay couples, churches tacitly communicate one message: *We want you to fail.*

No doubt some conservative Christians will own up to that assertion. Because they see our relationships as contrary to God's design, they may, indeed, want us to fail. That's at least honest, but undeniably cruel. Isn't there something tragic and mean-spirited about hoping for the demise of a relationship that is otherwise healthy and fruitful? Then what about moderate Christians who aren't sure if they agree with these relationships but have an open heart and don't want to seek their demise? The answer is easy: support and love these couples well. Even if you're uncertain about same-sex marriage, wouldn't it be wonderful if you could take a couple under your wing and help them to love each other more like Christ? Surely it seems more kind than shunning them and leaving them to struggle on their own. If you are clergy, consider offering marriage counseling to LGBTQ couples; try your best to edify the relationship. Dig deeply and intimately into their life together, and perhaps in doing so you'll get a better glimpse at what God is doing in their hearts.

Some may wonder what LGBTQ couples can do to seek out support in the church, but the responsibility for building supportive Christian communities rests on the shoulders of the majority. That is to say, it is time for straight Christians to step up to the plate and put their privilege to work. We can't ask queer couples to do all of the legwork here. The baggage many of us carry from the church, and the wounds around our sexuality that have left us hobbling, make navigating a young relationship hard enough. We may have the courage to step into church as a couple, but must we also fight for a seat at the table? There is a time and a place for engaging nonaffirming Christians; in fact, queer couples can be uniquely effective bridges between the church and the LGBTQ community. But if a church has any hope of engaging our community, its members must first make overtures of support and encouragement. At the very least, that church must be an environment where we're not forced to constantly justify the righteousness of our love.

If you're a queer couple attending a church that does not actively edify your relationship, it may be wise for you to leave. Maintain the friendships there that build you up, but don't waste your heart on leaders who are either too afraid or too hard-hearted to celebrate the whole of your humanity. Seek church and community elsewhere. Our pastor at Pearl Church in Portland likes to point out that the word *salvation* shares a root with the word *salve*. That, he reminds us often, is our true call as Christians: we are to be salves for the wounds of the injured. If the company of fellow believers feels instead like salt, don't be afraid to seek *salve-ation* elsewhere, even if it's among nonbelievers. Many of us have found that the secular community is better positioned to love us like Jesus than those who profess to follow him. Hold steadfast to your faith and to the knowledge that God smiles upon your relationship, but remember that pastors and churches don't have a monopoly on God's love.

Doing Better by Single People

LGBTQ couples are not the only islands in the church archipelago. As we open our hearts to these neglected couples, let us be mindful not to leave behind those who either by choice or circumstance remain single. Church culture has not always been a good environment for single people — unless we're talking about those who are young, straight, and looking for a mate. The church's neglect of single people is a sore spot for queer folks who have already become alienated from family and other sources of companionship. Many gay Christians have heeded the advice of the church to commit to a life of celibacy, only to find themselves sidelined for their singleness. It feels like being punished for playing by the rules.

The singleness stigma hits close to home for many straight Christians as well. Some years ago, our family celebration at Christmas included a friend who was a missionary overseas throughout her twenties and thirties. She has lived an exemplary, self-giving Christian life. She was enrolled in seminary that year, and discerning a call to ministry, yet she confessed that she had been feeling burned out on church. She no longer felt sure she belonged — because she was single.

Upon returning to the United States from her most recent stint abroad, our friend tried to go back to her old church. Rather than finding a community that embraced and nurtured her, she found that those in leadership weren't sure what to do with her — and they told her as much. At forty years old, she wasn't young enough to bond and socialize with the "young singles" groups, and almost everyone her age was married. Furthermore, there were limits to how far women could advance in leadership. Members of her church community treated her with either a subtle condescension or misguided sympathy.

If the church fails at supporting straight congregants just because they don't conform to the traditional family model, what hope of support is there for LGBTQ couples? If our desire is for the church to get same-sex marriage right, we must also push for it to approach singleness as an equally valid life choice. People who have been divorced, single parents, unmarried couples living together, interfaith couples, and in some areas still, interracial couples, all face the stigma of a church obsessed with the traditional family unit. We must work to bring all of them into the fold. Not only are they all deserving of support, but they may be the ones most in need of it.

The one notable difference between LGBTQ couples and these other "relationship outcasts" is that the rest of them can still move toward marriage within the church (with the exception of divorced people in some denominations). When a church excludes LGBTQ Christians from marriage—or refuses to support their relationships, watching quietly as they fail to blossom—the consequences for them become dire. Celibacy is exacted upon gay Christians like a sentence. Lesbian and gay people are told they must avoid romantic love at all cost, and when they do as they are told—embracing a life of singleness—they find themselves abandoned, patronized, left to feel not only alone but also inferior. By cordoning off queer Christians in a pen of celibacy, too many legalistic Christians "tie up heavy burdens, hard to bear, and lay them on the shoulders of others; but they themselves are unwilling to lift a finger to move them" (Matt. 23:4).

If we want churches that are truer to the gospel—communities that better resemble the kingdom—we must pull marriage off the pedestal we've built for it. We must remember that our spouses do not complete us, because none of us is just a half. Singleness is not a failure. Marriage is not a prize. Unmarried people deserve our respect as equal children of God, whole in their own persons. Let us each seek the Spirit's advice for our life. Let us discover our gift, be it singleness or married life, without pressure and without bias. Then let us use that gift for the benefit of our community. And let us celebrate unmarried people and the important benchmarks in their lives with the same joy we celebrate weddings and anniversaries.

Talking to our friend that Christmas about her experience as an adult single woman in the church reminded me (Constantino) of the ten Christmases I spent alone prior to my engagement. LGBTQ people often find ourselves alone during holidays. The first few times this happened it was because I couldn't afford the time or money to make the trip home. Later it was because my parents' house no longer felt like home. This is something I know any queer person who has suffered alienation will understand.

Spending Christmas alone didn't make me particularly sad. It was never my preference, but as an introvert, I was able to create my own traditions and rituals. I crafted my own space to celebrate and honor the full range of my feelings. But different personalities react to these situations differently. There are many for whom Thanksgiving and Christmas comprise the most difficult season of the year.

The holidays are an example of those times when you're supposed to be with your kin, your people. Holidays are hard for those of us who've seen the bonds of kinship dissolve in our families because it's when our friends go home to theirs. In my years alone, I was sometimes invited to spend Christmas with friends' families. The invitations were gracious, and I received them with gratitude. But the feeling I couldn't express was that often those celebrations made me feel worse. Seeing families interact during the holidays was like watching someone eat cake while you're on a diet. Eventually I began to turn down those invitations.

Looking back, it is clear to me that the holidays didn't bring sadness into my life; they merely shed light on it. What I needed wasn't to not be alone for Christmas. What I needed was to not be alone, period. What I missed most during that decade was the feeling that I belonged somewhere—that I belonged *to someone*. What I wanted, you see, wasn't a good meal, presents, or an evening of fun. What I longed for but couldn't articulate was to have a celebration that felt mine; I didn't want to just share in someone else's. I needed to be with people who were *my* people. In short, I needed to be doing life with people year-round. I needed that ideal I've come to understand as church: a community that hopefully includes your family but goes beyond it. Now that I have those relationships in my church community, I understand how vital that support is. Kinship is not merely a couple or a family unit; kinship incorporates a community.

Being church means believing, fully, that we are all siblings in Christ. Supporting LGBTQ couples and those either gay or straight who remain single means more than just a kind invitation once a year. It means making a commitment to live with them in intentional community year round. It means creating an environment where everyone can have a celebration they can call their own on Christmas—a celebration to which none of us needs an invitation because our presence is assumed.

There is a precedent in queer culture for this sort of community. In the darkest days of the 1980s, the "house system" associated with ballroom drag competitions became a refuge for queer people of color who had nowhere else to turn. Youth who had been disowned by their birth families and who fell victim to ostracism due to their race, gender identity, or sexual orientation, found support and acceptance in the social networks they encountered at clubs and in the streets. They were outcasts who banded together in order to survive in cities like New York and San Francisco. Older performers took on the role of "drag mothers," taking younger queens under their wing, mentoring them, and even offering many of them a roof. The groups established houses, often named after the mother's drag persona. These houses became chosen families that gave their members a sense of belonging. As Christians, we have much to learn about Christ from these even more marginalized siblings.

Kinship, we're beginning to understand, doesn't have to be limited to your spouse, parents, and children. Kinship can, and perhaps should, be an element of church itself. In 2 Samuel 5:1 we read that "all the tribes of Israel came to David at Hebron, and said, 'Look, we are your bone and flesh.'" They declared themselves kin to a man with whom many shared neither direct blood nor marriage ties. It is this greater kinship that ought to unite us to every member of our church—regardless of marital status and, for those who are married, regardless of the gender of their spouse. Only then will the church truly form a circle of support that protects and celebrates each other. In this new view of kinship, marriage emerges not as something couples seek only for their own fulfillment, but as the framework that allows them to better serve their community.

Church culture must change, and queer people can begin this reformation by remaining present—even as they enter into relationships and marriages—to those in their community who either by choice or circumstance remain single. Couples that have reached a place of stability in their relationship can become the support for others that they didn't have themselves. The LGBTQ community today suffers from a scarcity of elders. The generation that preceded us was decimated by the AIDS epidemic, and that has left us as orphans of sorts. We can honor those who lost their lives by supporting each other the way they did when society shunned them at their hour of greatest need. Just like they became family for each other, we can now be one another's church. We can discern together the wisdom we could have gained from the forebears we lost. Secure and established queer couples can be anchor posts for their single friends as they go out and navigate the choppy waters of dating. Groups of single folks can be that for each other as well. We've seen it happen among groups in New York, Los Angeles, Dallas, Atlanta, and Portland.

These cities all foster groups of queer Christians who have organized in response to the church's alienation. They share meals, organize small group meetings, and plan Bible studies—all of them outside of the framework of a formal church. They have done it without pastors or elders. They have created church simply by loving each other and trusting that the Divine is found where two or more gather in God's name.

Questions for Reflection

1. Do you believe you need community for your relationship to thrive? Why or why not?
2. If you're in a relationship, do you feel supported by your family and the church? How have they let you down, and what can they do better?
3. Have allies ever supported you even at the risk of being rejected themselves by church, family, or friends? What was that experience like for you?
4. Have you grown up with the message that married people have "achieved" something that other people have not? Does part of you still believe that?
5. What is the experience of being single in the church, or single among a group of mostly married friends? How could we be better at celebrating those who are single?
6. If you struggle with finding support, how can you "create church" outside of the system?

〜〜

LIVING AS BI WHEN YOUR MARRIAGE LOOKS STRAIGHT

Rosemary Jones found the support she needed not in the church but in her husband. As a cisgender woman married to a cisgender man, it would be seemingly easy for Rosemary to ignore or deny her sexuality. The two have a daughter and are active in their community. By the looks of it, their opposite-sex marriage is what you'd expect from the majority of the population. Yet you can't say they're in a straight marriage because, although Rosemary's husband is straight, she is not—she's bisexual. Theirs is a different kind of queer marriage than what most people expect when they hear the term, and therein lies the challenge.

The "B" in LGBTQ has long been the forgotten middle sibling in the queer community. Everyone includes it out of habit, but few pay much mind to it. Bi people, perhaps more than any other segment of the queer community, find themselves having to defend their identity even within LGBTQ circles. "Being bi—and specifically, being bi with an opposite-gender partner—means I am too queer for straight spaces and too straight for queer spaces," Rosemary says. "Going into a gay bar with my husband could be greeted with all the side-eye and annoyance over straight-crashers. Mentioning my bisexuality in hetero, churched spaces is sometimes greeted with discomfort and inappropriate questions about our marriage and sex life. They'd all be far more comfortable if I would just remain silent. It doesn't confuse them if I let my partner create my visibility."

Rosemary first came out when she was a teenager in the 1990s. She had been raised in a conservative Christian home by a very religious mother and was steeped in evangelical purity culture. "By the time I was about fifteen, I knew that I was bi," she says, "and for a number of reasons felt that I needed to distance myself from the church as much as possible." She spent the next decade openly identifying as bi, and in terms of faith, she became agnostic. "The problem," she says, "is that during that period I also engaged in a lot of dysfunctional behaviors. And after about ten years I hit a bottom. At that point, the pendulum swung back far into the fundamentalist faith of my childhood, because that was all that I knew. I just assumed that in order to get sober and clean I also needed to put a lid on my sexuality. Being bi got lumped in with everything else, as if just saying I was bi meant I had to also be an addict or engage in unhealthy behaviors."

Rosemary put herself back in the closet and embraced the language of fundamentalism. "If I ever spoke about it," she says, "it was only to say that it was something God had healed me from." That season took up the next ten years of her life. During that time, and in that context, she met her husband, Josh. "We met at our old church, and he had also been raised very conservatively—homeschooled, everything," she says. "But by the time we met, we had both started moving slowly towards a more progressive Christianity."

When things started getting serious with Josh, Rosemary knew she had to tell him about her past. He wasn't fazed, but she still carried deep shame about it. "Internally, there were still these moments of attraction to other women," she says, "and it was debilitating. It was so crippling. We would be out on a date, and I would think our waitress was cute. And something like that—which for other people would just be a fleeting thought that they would notice and let it go—for me, it became something I would notice, and then I'd spiral. I'd start thinking, 'Why hasn't God healed me? What is wrong with me?' You know, in our generation we were taught that it was demonic possession, or a sign that something was broken in me. So I would start thinking that I was going to ruin my marriage, and that my husband would be so disappointed if he knew."

The spiral would go on for weeks, and then depression and anxiety would kick in. It was tortuous, but eventually she would work up the courage to confess to Josh. The way he responded was the salve she needed for true healing to take place. "Every time he was floored that I'd be in such anguish over this," she says. "He would be like, 'Oh yeah, I remember her; she was cute.' He just didn't see the need for me to be ashamed and so hard on myself."

For years, they would go through this cycle, with Rosemary unable to bring herself to address it directly. Rosemary remembers the night they finally talked openly about it: "We sat on the couch, he looked me in the eye, and said, 'You know what? I really, really love having a bisexual wife.' And I'd never used that word to identify myself to him. I hadn't used that word in ten years. I just cried. It was like a dam had burst. I knew I could come out."

That kind of safety in marriage is what we all hope for regardless of our sexual orientation and regardless of what boogeymen lurk in the gardens of our imagination. But for an invisible sexual minority like bi people, it's not easy to find. A straight spouse who hasn't experienced the anguish of the closet might have trouble understanding the need of a bi person to come out. "People have told me that I have a certain privilege because I can pass as straight," says Rosemary. "I'm married to a man. I have a kid and a fairly basic suburban life. But if you ask any woman in my situation, she will tell you that there's really two sides to that coin, because you can call it a privilege or call it being closeted. So the real question is, do you feel like that's comforting, or is it stifling?"

Rosemary found the experience stifling, and coming out publicly has made both her life and her marriage richer. "My favorite thing about marriage is always having a partner, a best friend, having someone who understands me and is striving to understand me. Being known has brought us so much closer together."

To Rosemary, part of being known is being seen. She's an artist, and much of her work explores living in the in-between, of not fitting neatly into one category. Being bisexual, says Rosemary, is about more than who she finds attractive: "It informs my art, it informs my politics, my relationships, my friendships. Being out and being vocal about it has given me the freedom to engage the world in a richer, deeper, more authentic way than if I continued to use a filter by playing straight."

A motif of some of her artwork is the color purple, a blend of the more common colors blue and pink. Together, these colors make up the bisexual pride flag.

"I like how [trans writer and speaker] Austen Hartke put it in one of his YouTube videos. He was speaking about the spectrum of gender, but I associate it with orientation, talking about how in the beginning God created night and day, but God also created dawn and dusk. God created land and water, but God also created shore and marsh. Being bisexual allows me to live in and appreciate those in-between spaces, being able to pick out beauty and nuance in ways that are often missed by people who only see the binary."

Rosemary's marriage advice:
"Grow together. Give each other room to grow, but as much as you can, try to always stay connected on that growth. Don't leave each other behind."

CHAPTER 6

———————— ∽∾∽ ————————

ENGAGEMENT PAINS

Neither of us ever thought we'd get married. Because we grew up in the 1980s and '90s, the notion of someday marrying a guy never even crossed our minds. And at some level we knew, even when we were young, that marrying a woman wouldn't be the best idea. The movement for marriage equality picked up some steam when we were in our mid-twenties, but even then, the thought of it someday being the law of the land seemed like a distant possibility.

We had been dating for close to a year when the landmark Supreme Court ruling *Obergefell v. Hodges* was decided. The fact that our relationship was going so well and the realization that we could legally get married anywhere in this country got us thinking for the first time, well into our thirties, about the meaning of marriage. What was the point of marriage? Was it an outdated institution? Even if it still had relevance, was marriage right for us?

The conversations were a bit awkward at first, and purely theoretical. We talked about how, if any two people (not necessarily us, of course!) got married, it should be for reasons that go beyond selfish wants. We both liked the idea of a marriage that, rather than turning inward and only serving each other, strengthened and filled us up as individuals so that we could ultimately turn outward.

Constantino, ever the fan of ancient Greece, brought up Homer. He talked about Odysseus's first encounter with a mortal after seven years of captivity on Calypso's island. That person was a young woman named Nausicaa, daughter of the king of the Phaeacians. Nausicaa was of marrying age and eager to find a husband. Odysseus, still deeply in love with his wife, Penelope, took the opportunity to share his views on marriage. Like-mindedness, he told Nausicaa, is a married couple's best claim to glory. Possessing two minds that work as one makes the pair a joy to their friends, a sorrow to their enemies.

Constantino pointed out that Homer used that passage to highlight a truth we risk forgetting today: Marriage is not all about love. Marriage, Homer seemed to be saying, goes beyond feelings, and it transcends even the couple themselves. A good marriage brings joy also to those around it.

Of course, marriage has served many purposes throughout history. For centuries, marriage was all about property, politics, and money. It helped men gain lands, build wealth, and make alliances. As for women, it offered a means of security and protection, while simultaneously being a tool for their control and subjugation. Contemporary Christian culture has come to understand marriage as being exclusively about family and having a framework for raising children (it's no wonder one of conservative Christianity's most powerful organizations is called Focus on the Family). Whether or not we agree with these purposes, they all share one characteristic: they make marriage about something greater than the desires and emotions of the couple involved.

The slogan of the marriage equality movement, "Love Wins," offers a tender but perhaps myopic view of married life. In reading the Gospels, we hear Jesus—who was love made flesh—teaching that the point of marriage is not love but the establishment of kinship. He said that it was people's desire to create that proverbial one-flesh bond with another that leads them to leave the home where they were raised and to start a new one. He used this framework to set narrow rules for divorce, thus confirming that marriage concerns more than the two people directly involved.

Early Christian thinkers developed their own ideas about the purpose of marriage, some of them framing it as a way of preventing sin. Informed by Paul's assertion in 1 Corinthians 7:9 that "it is better to marry than to be aflame with passion," Augustine came to see marriage as a handicap—a crutch for those of us who are so weak that we can't control our sex drive. Thomas Aquinas's view was more nuanced, informed by Aristotle's view of marriage as the foundation of a virtuous society. Aquinas believed the institution of marriage was grounded in natural law and was crucial for the establishment of family and the upbringing of children.

The two of us eventually landed on an understanding of marriage informed by all of these thinkers but based primarily on the teachings of Jesus. We think marriage is ultimately about the establishment of kinship and about the obligations that come with it. Love plays a critical role in marriage, and it has remained a cornerstone of ours. But we knew, even back when were just two lovebirds getting to know each other, that it is not enough for the long haul. We talk a lot about kinship because we are convinced that it is that bond—the notion that another person can be your flesh and bone—that establishes a marriage's foundation.

But don't accept our definition of marriage as gospel. Take the time to consider what marriage means to you. If you're in a relationship that is moving toward marriage or you're aspiring to be, ask yourself why. We've seen too many friends, straight and gay, move mindlessly toward their nuptials without considering whether it was the best path for them. Romantic relationship should never be the default destination. If you want marriage primarily to fill a void, ask yourself what that emptiness is and whether a spouse can truly and fully fill it. If you're seeking marriage to chase a vision of what life should be, talk to friends who are married to see what aspects of that dream come true and which are mere fantasy. Being thoughtful as a couple about not only why you're getting married but what you want your relationship to look like is the first step toward the like-mindedness Homer encouraged and the subsequent joy it will yield for years to come.

Having spent many hours over the course of many months philosophizing about marriage, we knew our days of just dating were coming to an end. We had both left our homes and settled in a new city to be with each other. We'd had long, awkward conversations about our finances and spending habits. We'd had painful, vulnerable conversations about our pasts. We had fought and reconciled. We had imagined life single, and though we'd both been amenable to that in the past, getting to know each other had rendered that a much less appealing prospect. We realized, as we began doing life together, that we wanted to continue doing exactly that.

I (Constantino) had told David that, since it was he who had the most reservations about God's plans for same-sex relationships, it should be he who proposed. There are no rules or expectations about these things when you're a same-sex couple. But I've never valued patience as a virtue. When I came across an Airbnb listing of a fire lookout tower tucked away in a remote forest, I booked it six months in advance, knowing that if David hadn't proposed by then, I would make my move.

We rented a car and drove four hours south of Portland, toward Crater Lake, a sapphire blue body of water created by the collapse of the ancient volcano Mount Mazama. David had no idea where we were going and even less of a clue of what was in store. It was early November 2015, and we had been Oregon residents for just under six months. We didn't expect to find snow on some parts of the road that early in the year, but the white-dusted trees along the way lent the drive an air of magic that would last the whole trip.

Darkness enveloped us as we approached our destination. The tower was off the grid, so we couldn't rely on Google Maps to reach it. We drove slowly along the dark gravel roads, under thick canopies of trees. The spooky scene was perfect for a horror film, and we mused about what we would do if an eerie-looking girl suddenly appeared in the middle of the desolate road. "Run her over!" said David. Not five seconds later, a deer leapt onto our path. We both screamed louder than the little girl of our imagination ever would. But we avoided the accident, and heart palpitations soon gave way to laughter.

We reached our hosts' property and drove up a narrow road to an expansive prairie, the sea of trees receding behind us. The tower stood in the center, warm and inviting above us, like a cloud on fire. We truly were in the proverbial middle of nowhere—and we loved it. The following day was glorious. We took in the cold air and watched the clouds roll over the prairie, washing over the forest below. We soaked in a wood fire-heated hot tub, read, and napped to the sound of rain on the metal roof.

For dinner, I changed into a nice sweater and a bow tie. Only then did David grow suspicious. The sky had been overcast since we arrived, but when we went out onto the balcony after dinner, we found ourselves covered not by a blanket of clouds but of brilliant stars. It was as if God were smiling on us, opening a window into heaven. Our hosts, who lived nearby and knew of my plans, had offered to drive to the other side of the forest and light some floating Chinese lanterns. David, being appropriately vigilant atop a fire lookout tower, thought it might be a forest fire and wondered aloud if we shouldn't get help. But when he turned away from the view, he saw me kneeling before him.

Holding two cross pendants, engraved with each other's initials, I mumbled something about our shared faith, and asked, "Will you help me bear my cross? Will you let me share yours? Will you marry me?" David, who has trouble buying a jar of salsa without careful consideration, murmured a nervous yes. We placed the crosses around each other's necks and wore them for the rest of our engagement.

We soon started laughing. For two guys who avoid anything saccharine and schmaltzy, the whole thing was embarrassingly romantic. Then we cried, because, well, *feelings*. And then we laughed again. During a more serious moment, David looked me in the eye, took my hand, and spoke the words we shared in the introduction: "I will be your family. I will be yours, and you will no longer be alone. I never want to hear you say you're alone again."

Those words touched me in a way I didn't expect. Something in my life changed at that moment. I sobbed, and let all my weight fall on David's shoulder. He wrapped his arms around me and held me tighter than I'd ever been held. For years, I had lived as if I had no kin, and this moment, on a cold night in the middle of nowhere, felt like coming home.

Releasing Hope of Reconciliation

That feeling of coming home was abruptly interrupted in the following days. Unbeknownst to us that night, our move toward creating a bond of kinship would cause to resurface the broken bonds between me and my family. My parents and siblings were the first people with whom I shared the news of my engagement to David. I barely got a signal in that fire lookout tower, but the next morning I waved my phone around in the air until the message to my family finally went through. Two of my three sisters, my brother, niece, and nephews all expressed support and happiness for me. Those two sisters even came to our wedding.

My parents and my oldest sister, however, didn't even acknowledge it was happening. From what I was told, my parents didn't outwardly object ("Whatever makes him happy," my mom told one of my sisters). But they said nothing to me upon our engagement—not "Congratulations," and not even "Don't do this." I called them a couple of weeks later, on my dad's birthday, after barely sleeping the night before. We talked for more than thirty minutes. We talked about the weather where I live and the weather where they live. We talked about the presidential race. We talked about world politics, and the danger of a new world war. We talked about their health. We joked. We even talked about a distant cousin whose name I didn't recognize. And then—never acknowledging the engagement—we said a pleasant goodbye.

That weekend, David saw me cry as he never had before. A week later I was still crying. He met me at work one day during my lunch break, and we went for a walk. On the eastern shore of the Willamette River, fifteen miles from where he eventually became my next of kin, he held me as I gave up hope of retrieving the kinship I had lost.

I wonder if what I say about my family will ever be entirely fair coming from only one point of view. It's hard to be objective when writing about something that touches the core of who you've been. The truth is that though almost two decades have passed since I first came out to my parents, the feelings surrounding our relationship are still raw.

But I know I'm not the only person whose relationship with his parents has collapsed. Others with broken family bonds should know that they are not alone, because imagining our pain to be unique does little to heal it.

When I came out to my parents, they didn't try to change me. They didn't issue ultimatums. They didn't disown me. They simply decided that I, as I am, do not exist. That shallow phone conversation after my engagement hurt because it was a reminder that, to them, I have ceased to be a person worth knowing. We received a wedding gift from my mother, but to this day, I'm not even sure my father knows I was ever engaged, much less married. (He has a health condition that makes it difficult to communicate over the phone.) My life has moved on. David and I bought a house. We might someday have children. And I can't talk to them about any of this.

Had my parents and oldest sister rejected me outright, I would have found it easier to grieve. Rejection is a subverted form of relationship—a connection based on opposition. Instead, their indifference made me feel like a nonentity. For a decade and a half, our relationship had been like a patient with a degenerative disease. By the time I got engaged, the relationship was still breathing, but in a vegetative state.

Some people try to be encouraging by offering platitudes such as "While there is life, there is hope." I understand that sentiment, because losing hope feels like death. And like death, we are told to avoid it. But I think this advice is wrong. Too often we cling to hope for dear life, even when it makes life unbearable. Like the death of someone who is suffering, relinquishing hope can mean relief. Unreasonable hope—wishing to change that which can't be changed—becomes a black hole that sucks the joy out of everything it touches.

Losing hope of having a relationship with my parents was hard, because things weren't always bad. I had a happy childhood and an authentic relationship with both of them. But they are the product of a world where appearances are king, where the family name gets placed on a pedestal. Their society has made conformity an idol, and having an openly gay child is embarrassing.

I believe my parents would be fine with me being gay—being in a relationship, even—if only I kept it secret. It hurt when I first realized this, because it means that they care more about what others think than they do about me. I know they are as heartbroken about the way things have turned out as I am, but their society's idol demanded a sacrifice, and there were only two lambs: my happiness and our relationship. When I could not offer the former, I slew the latter.

Hope is not lost in one day. It's not lost in a conversation or after a single event. Hope is lost slowly, over the course of many years. It is lost after repeated blows. I tried for a long time to include my parents in my life. I will never forget the last time my parents visited me in New York, in 2006. They refused to set foot in my apartment, where I lived with my long-term partner. They resisted even coming to my neighborhood. At one point during the trip, my father said to me, "We have done enough all these years trying to pretend you're normal. You cannot ask more of us." My mom acquiesced with her silence.

A few days later I wrote them a letter that I never sent. "I am your son," I wrote, "and you refused to set foot in my apartment; you wouldn't even visit my neighborhood. You tell me you're merely 'trying to pretend' I'm normal, with no regard to how hurtful that is. And then you expect me to be grateful for that. What you're telling me is that I can't ask you to be a part of my life and that I can't expect you to ever try to understand me." I had been *emotionally* disowned. I was left feeling as if I had no kin.

I tried again in 2011, a year that changed the course of my life. I wrote (and mailed) them a long letter, fully baring my heart. They received it but never acknowledged it. A few months into my relationship with David, I told my mom about him. I said things could develop into something serious. She showed no interest in learning who he was or what he was like. Again, it made me feel as if I had no family.

As we wrote in our introduction, a person without kin is alone at a primal level—an aloneness God recognized in Genesis 2:18 as "not good." Kinship is a bond based on shared experience and a shared identity that distinguishes you and your people from the rest of the world. When the parent-child bond breaks, it damages every relationship built around it. The breakdown of my relationship with my parents distanced me from my siblings as well. Even the three of my siblings who have kept in touch have trouble wrapping their heads around my loss, and they often get caught in the void that now exists between my parents and me. Some of them have tried to be bridges, but the gap is too wide for any of them to cover.

I believe kinship is a gift from God. To establish it, he gave us the gifts of child rearing and marriage. I lost that bond with the people who reared me and with whom I grew up. I was able to give up hope of reestablishing it because in David I have a new family. He is my kin now, and I can't keep allowing myself to be erased.

The house that nurtured me as a child is in ruins, but among those ruins are beautiful memories. I will hold on to them. I've shared some with David, and if we decide to become parents, I will share them with my children. I love my mom and dad dearly, and I know they are honorable. I know they did their best. I can be at peace now as I build this new house.

Many who relate to my story also know that you can't help but feel guilt when you give up on your parents. The consequences might affect the rest of your family. That, I guess, is when you turn to Christ. Don't relinquish hope in haste; don't relinquish it if it's merely to serve yourself. But don't make senseless hope an idol. Don't let it drive you away from God. Don't let it leave you useless to others.

When Someone Points the Finger of Sin

I (David) was fortunate enough to keep my relationship with my family. Although they had trouble adjusting to the news of our marriage, there was never a risk of us losing relationship entirely. My relationship with Constantino might have seemed strange and embarrassing to them, but my brave family always chose to love first. My friends, however, were a mixed bag.

Only a couple of months into our engagement, I received an email from a friend at my old church who pointed the finger of sin at me. He expressed his grave disapproval for our choice to marry and offered an earnest appeal for me to "come to my senses." He likened my faith to a frog in a pot of heating water: I had been changing my theology by degree so gradually that I couldn't see how I was warping my faith to serve my own selfish desires and not God's.

The email hurt; it triggered all of my past shame, anger, fear. I was about to embark upon the biggest decision of my life, and someone was trying to insert doubt into my choice. I received the email while we were at the annual conference of Q Christian Fellowship, the leading non-profit offering support and conversation around issues of sexuality and faith. Being there, I think, was serendipitous. Feeling God's presence alive and moving in a space of more than a thousand LGBTQ Christians helped remind me how misguided that email was.

How do we respond when someone calls us a sinner during one of the most joyous moments of our lives? I knew it was a possibility in some of my conservative faith circles, but I was so caught up in the moment that I hadn't prepared emotionally.

I spent days thinking up all sorts of sassy retorts (there were many; none were sent). I decided it would be fruitless to try to change my friend's mind, especially through an email exchange. All I could do was manage my response, both outwardly and inwardly. I replied with a polite but concise email, thanking him for caring enough to reach out but insisting my faith was as informed as his.

The engagement of an LGBTQ couple will almost certainly spark conversation in conservative faith communities. My takeaway from the interaction with my disapproving friend was to learn who to invest energy in and who to ignore. The extent to which we engage with friends and family about our engagement depends on the roles they play in our lives.

The problem with my casual friend was that we didn't have any real relationship. He's a sweet guy and a true lover of Jesus, but we were never close enough to speak meaningfully into each other's lives. He hadn't gotten to know Constantino and had never spent time with us to see the fruit borne of our relationship. So when he wrote me with his Scripture-spattered disapproval, my heart had little generosity to listen. Furthermore, his message consisted of nothing more than the same tired clobber passages from the Bible with which I was all too well acquainted. I had wrestled with the issue of homosexuality for twenty years—through agonizing therapy, scholarly books, thoughtful discussion, Bible study, and endless prayer. I doubt he had been so diligent about the issue. So when he asserted my wrongness with so much confidence, it felt to me like an insolent kindergartener criticizing a PhD's solution to a calculus problem.

Constantino and I had closer friends at our old church who expressed reservations about our relationship, but my heart was far more attuned to their concerns. The difference was that I trusted their words as being spoken with love and a desire to understand, and not with the hubris of righteousness. These friends loved me first, and only then offered their reservations. Although I ultimately felt confident about moving forward in our marriage, I took these friends' concerns to heart, and our relationships remain intact. The lesson for all of us is this: your authority to speak into someone's life is directly proportional to your investment in the relationship.

Even though I had worked through all of my doubts about same-sex relationship, the experience made me second-guess whether I was keeping an ear open to God or, as my casual friend suggested, pursuing my own selfish desires. But remaining open to God's voice does not mean revisiting a difficult decision every time someone raises questions about it. I had worked through this long and complex problem about my sexuality many, many times and was satisfied with the answers God had given me. Trying to solve the same problem over and over again is not only futile but destructive. It wouldn't serve our marriage today if I questioned its spiritual validity every time someone sent us a nasty email. I believe God led us to this marriage, and so I have to trust that God will see us through it.

Getting married requires drawing a healthy boundary around your relationship to protect it from those who would poke and prod at it. When we received uncharitable comments while we were dating, I passively ignored them and let them slough off me. Our engagement season was the first time I realized that I needed to be firm in defending our relationship. If I wasn't resolute, I would open myself back up to the doubt and shame I worked so hard to get past.

The decision to get married is one no couple should take lightly. But when you are in a relationship that transgresses society's norms—when you're LGBTQ, when you date outside your race or social class, and even when you date someone who doesn't share your family's religion—the choice to get married comes with consequences that others never face. If this is the kind of marriage upon which you're embarking, allow yourself the time to discern carefully what marriage is and why you want it. Be confident in your decision and ready to defend it. Then rest in the knowledge that the partner you have chosen is the right one to face the fallout with you. If relationships become strained or damaged, you'll have that thoughtful decision to lean on and carry you through.

That's not to say we shouldn't mourn the relationships we lose. Many of us will have a loved one who rejects or shuns us when we step into marriage, and the loss can be as real as death. Allow space for the grief of losing parts of your past that you have loved. Mourn for as long as you need to mourn. And when you're ready to stand, face the future with the joy of knowing that God has gifted you with new kin.

Questions for Reflection

1. Marriage has served many purposes throughout history. What does it mean to you?
2. What kind of engagement traditions are meaningful to you, and which would you throw out?
3. Has your relationship forced your church or other people in your life to take a stand on LGBTQ issues one way or another? What happened, and how did you respond?
4. Who is "kin" for you right now? How has your sexuality or gender identity affected the bond of kinship with your family?
5. At what point, if ever, should we release the hope of restoring relationship with someone who has rejected us?

CHAPTER 7

─────── ∞⁓∞ ───────

THE BRIDELESS
WEDDING

One of the aspects of same-sex marriage we appreciate most is the freedom it affords us to deconstruct the
cultural traditions that weigh down the wedding experience. After all, once you've subtracted a bride or groom
from the equation, pretty much anything goes. Grandma
isn't going to sweat the small stuff, like whether you'll be
throwing a bouquet.

When we began planning our wedding, we looked forward to all of the ways we could slough off traditional
expectations: No resentful groomsmen in two-hundred-
dollar rented tuxes. No drunken bachelor parties in Mex-
ico or Las Vegas. No adorable flower girls plopping down
rose petals as if the queen of Sheba had come to town.

We stripped out the cake, the bridal shower, the proces-
sion, and those disgusting perennial wedding favors known
as Jordan almonds. After we removed the parties, the des-
serts, and the customs, we felt safe that we had avoided getting caught up in the corporate wedding machine, despite
the onslaught of Facebook ads we received for bridal expos

and local jewelers. But stripping out everything also left us feeling empty.

A number of people offered to throw us engagement parties, but we politely declined. We figured the wedding was celebration enough. Fortunately, we have some awesome friends who decided to throw engagement parties for us anyway. During a trip to Los Angeles a few months before our wedding, the home group that David used to host for our old church turned a casual reunion into an amazing engagement party. A few days later, David's sister planned a brunch with his cousins so they could meet Constantino and learn the good news of our engagement. We left both of these events feeling full. While many traditions are pointless, over the top, or commercially driven, we realized that some do have a purpose. They serve as a public declaration of commitment, faith, and love, and they invite others to share in your joy.

During our engagement, we struggled with feeling as if our upcoming wedding was inferior, as if it was somehow "playing house" compared to opposite-sex weddings. This was in part because of the tepid response we had received from some friends and family. Perhaps we were afraid to be too enthusiastic because it would only highlight those in our lives who were not. But it was also because, in eschewing tradition, we weren't approaching our wedding with the fanfare most ceremonies receive.

Don't downplay your wedding just because traditions feel too conventional or heteronormative. We learned that if you throw out all the customs, the event stops looking like a celebration of marriage altogether. A wedding stripped of all tradition, ceremony, and rituals is just a signed certificate at a courthouse. It's official, but it lacks the commemoration and reverence to mark one of life's greatest decisions.

Traditions, however, are a double-edged sword. At their best they reinforce meaning, and at their worst they pervert it. Traditions become empty when we mindlessly go through the motions without knowing why. Why is there a best man? Why do brides wear a white dress? Why is there a garter and bouquet toss? Traditions have also been used to harm and denigrate. For example, we might argue that the tradition of the father giving away the bride, as sweet as it looks, perpetuates a patriarchal framework in which women are essentially property.

For this reason, all couples, but especially LGBTQ couples, may be well served to dissect the elements of a wedding and ask critical questions: What genuinely matters to us in the act of marriage? Which traditions are meaningless or offensive? What traditions do we want to introduce? How can we imbue new meaning into old traditions? What nuptial elements honor our relationship or reflect Christ?

Meaningful traditions ground us in our identities. They remind us of who we are and where we came from. These might include cultural elements or traditions unique to your family. They might mean honoring special people in your lives who have supported your relationship. They might simply mean doing something silly and fun during your wedding because that's you, and doing so would honor your relationship.

Ultimately, we reached a good middle ground. We threw out the silly stuff, but we brought back historical traditions, such as having guests sign a wedding covenant as witnesses to our vows and having our sisters place a wedding cord over our shoulders to symbolize our union. The wedding wasn't as stripped down or avant-garde as we originally had hoped, but it echoed the joy and sanctity of the ceremony that has threaded marriages throughout time. And, most important, there were no Jordan almonds.

The Engagement "Ick" Emergency

I (David) wanted to be married—I just didn't want to *get* married. I had grown accustomed to dating a man and was finally comfortable in my own skin, but the prospect of a same-sex wedding triggered all of my past insecurities like a floor full of sprung mousetraps. One of my first thoughts after accepting Constantino's proposal was "How can I work this so that we get married but don't actually have a ceremony?"

My faith in the sanctity of our relationship didn't dispel the recurring "ick" factor that had become so deeply ingrained in my psyche. I struggled with how to cope with this feeling without consistently isolating and rejecting my would-be husband. I knew an important part of this was communicating my feelings. In moments when I have tried to hide the ick, Constantino still has picked up on it and interpreted it as rejection. When I was able to verbalize my repulsion, he was intuitive enough to give me space when I needed it or lean in to help me push through it.

It was a five-alarm ick emergency the week we got engaged. The first image that came to mind was a wedding cake topper—that plastic thing you put on top of a cake—with two grooms. I had seen some with grooms that looked like the "twinsies" I so feared, with matching tuxedos and plastic smiles painted on their soulless faces. They were silly and trivial, and yet somehow the thought of them triggered in me all of my unresolved unease with my own gay relationship.

When I got home from the wonderful weekend in which we got engaged, I went straight to the computer and googled images of gay wedding cakes. I'm a masochist that way. I imagined myself as that cake topper, a painted smile on my face, standing next to my twin, and it disturbed me. Also, I hate cake.

I finally told Constantino that although I was honored and excited to marry him, I couldn't stand the idea of a wedding. I would do anything to avoid a ceremony—to escape aisles and altars and pastel-colored flower bouquets.

What Constantino pointed out to me was perhaps the most obvious and revolutionary idea during our engagement. When I described to him my nightmare vision of matching outfits and scented candles and Shania Twain's "From This Moment" blasting as we marched down the aisle, he simply said, "But that's not you. That's not us." And it was true. Even if I were marrying a woman, I wouldn't want white rose centerpieces and a string quartet. I wouldn't want perfumed invitations or spring color schemes (not when I'm clearly an autumn). I would feel uncomfortable with those ceremonial aesthetics regardless of the person standing next to me at the altar.

So when I felt icky looking at photos of other gay weddings—whether it was grooms with matching rainbow suspenders or napkins monogrammed *Mr. & Mr.*—I reminded myself that that's not me. It was someone else's style and someone else's vision of romance, and it was all perfectly wonderful. But it wasn't me. And that was OK.

A big pitfall in relationships is to compare yours to other people's, or to develop a belief about what your marriage "should" look like. Every relationship has its own way of being in the world: its own internal culture, its own ways of navigating conflict, its own personality. The mistake I was making in envisioning our wedding was that I was overlaying another relationship's personality onto ours. It felt wrong because it *was* wrong. Every couple finds its own unique way to function, and while we can pick up tips from others, no two will be perfectly alike. This is a lesson many of us need to learn time and again.

Early in our relationship, when I was feeling especially icky one night about dating a man, Constantino said to me, "I wish you could stop focusing on the fact that I'm a man. Just think of me as Tino." It made all the difference. I discovered that when I removed the abstract concepts and the preconceived notions, the cultural norms and the disembodied visions of myself, the ickiness went away. I was just David. He was just Constantino. And we were just two people getting married.

One Bridge, Two Lives

We got married outdoors in May, under a bridge in Portland. The day could not have been more beautiful: gray and chilly, with bouts of soft rain. It may not have been what most people would call great wedding weather, but it was perfect for *our* wedding. The days leading up were sunny and hot, but the temperature dropped thirty degrees overnight and by Saturday, May 14, the clouds had rolled in. We may have been a little worried about guests getting wet, but a rainy wedding was our secret joy and hope. As a relationship that hasn't conformed to expectations in so many ways, the weather was the appropriate reflection of us. It was as if God had smiled on us again and said, "I know you, and this is the day I made for you. This day will feel like you."

After months of discussion and apprehension about mindless conventions and irrelevant societal norms, what did our wedding look like? Ultimately, it looked a lot like a wedding. We wanted to honor tradition, but not without examining it. We didn't want to be pointedly different; we just wanted to be genuine. Every tradition and word allowed in our ceremony had been carefully vetted to make sure it was true to us.

This authenticity is perhaps the most refreshing aspect of the same-sex weddings we have attended. There is a freshness in them, a new life. Because LGBTQ couples have only had federal recognition of marriage in the United States since 2015, and because they have defied convention at every turn, these couples have looked at the institution of marriage with a more critical eye than most. They have had to want it more than most because they have had to risk and sacrifice more than most to get it. The same-sex weddings we've attended have had an aura of triumph about them as well as an air of celebration. Love is palpable at these ceremonies, not only between the two getting married but among the community surrounding them.

These weddings are about two people, but they are also about so much more.

Our ceremony was set in a park under the St. John's Bridge, between two massive pillars that reach toward each other until they join at the top to look like the pointed archway of a cathedral. A line of these arches continues along the bridge's belly, down a long grassy slope and across the Willamette River. It is a striking, mesmerizing view.

To honor our guests—and to avoid having all eyes on us—we had them process instead of us. This caught people by surprise, but it brought us great delight. We had each guest announced by name, and small groups walked down a long set of stairs toward the altar. There, standing by the Communion table, we took time to speak to each guest, telling them why it meant so much to us that they were there.

Tears flowed. The first group was our pastors, and David started choking up right away. By the time his high school friends came down, he was full on laugh-crying. He couldn't even speak! It fell on Constantino to tell them how beautiful it was that they have remained close all these decades. Constantino broke down when his sisters got to the front, crying the ugliest ugly-cry you can imagine. After so much family rejection, it was a moment of healing, and his heart burst as he held each of them tight. David's tears returned as soon as his parents, sister, and dogs started walking down. We felt God's presence in every hug.

The ceremony started with the words of creation: "Then the LORD God said, 'It's not good that the human is alone. I will make him a helper that is perfect for him'" (Gen. 2:18, CEB). That day, as we helped each other set up chairs, carry boxes, and finish the table decorations, we knew, better than ever, that we were the helpers best suited for each other. We didn't want to sit front and center, apart from our guests, so after Constantino read the verse, we took our seats with the rest of the congregation.

There is one tradition we revived that has generally fallen out of favor in contemporary weddings: the marriage objection. The words are famous and hackneyed, better suited these days to a punch line or a plot device in a movie: "If any of you can show just cause why these two may not be married under the laws of both God and man, speak now, or else forever hold your peace."

When we presented this language in advance to our pastor, who was presiding over the ceremony, he raised an eyebrow. "You feel comfortable doing this?" he asked. In all of the weddings over which he had presided, he had never spoken that language in a ceremony.

He was on board with our choice, but he wanted us to be ready for the possibility that someone actually would object. How would we handle that? Who would address the objection? What would we say? Did we have Tasers ready? It seemed as if we were inviting trouble. But to us, it was a crucial component in kicking off not only our wedding but our lives together.

Anyone who has been in a relationship that has faced resistance from the outside world—whether from friends, family, church, or culture—is familiar with the yearning for peace and closure. There's a desire to lay down weapons and put to rest all of the debate and opposition your relationship has caused. Whether it's a same-sex pairing; or a relationship of distinct classes, or races, or religions; or even couples embarking on second marriages, outside pressure can break a couple. A marriage, then, is a victory, a triumph between two people who have overcome not only external opposition but the obstacles of self to mutually submit to each other in a covenant between themselves and God.

The inclusion of this language was symbolic. It was a declaration that the battle was over, the war was won, and it was time for celebration. Among our inner circles, the final opportunity to speak out against our marriage was in essence a call for reconciliation. For those who love us most, this language was an appeal to them—and a promise by them—that from our wedding day forward, these people agreed to be our allies, not our enemies. They committed to being for us, not against us. When we asked sixty of our friends and family to "hold their peace," what we were really asking was for them to help us hold *our* peace, to help us hold together our union with the love and support only community can provide.

The words were spoken and there were, fortunately, no objections. David's family dog barked a lot, but we interpreted that as a vote of confidence.

With that past, we could enjoy one of the true highlights of the ceremony: the music. Our pastor of worship put together a ten-person choir and arranged three songs for us. The first song, immediately following the verse from Genesis, set the mood for celebration: Hall and Oates's "You Make My Dreams Come True." Then, as we knelt after the marriage, they blessed us by singing a prayer. They asked that God, who is Perfect Love and Perfect Life, grant us faith, hope, endurance, trust, and peace. The ceremony ended with a joyous rendition of "Oh Happy Day."

Jesus said, "Are you tired? Worn out? Burned out on religion? Come to me. Get away with me and you'll recover your life." He promised that if we keep company with him, we'll "learn to live freely and lightly" (Matt. 11:28–30, *The Message*).

That day, we wanted to experience with our friends what *The Message* translation of that Bible passage describes as "the unforced rhythms of grace." We wanted to remember that Jesus "won't lay anything heavy or ill-fitting" on us. Rather than have one person go up and read for a long time, we had a Gospel flash mob: a dozen friends stood up one by one and each read a verse.

For the vows, we kept the traditional formula. We liked what that structure said about the nature of Christian marriage and the elements of the covenant. We started by each making a promise to God to care for the other "in faithfulness and holiness of life." We then gave ourselves to one another, promising to endure all things and bear all things, in times of plenty and in times of want, and to forsake all others for as long as we both shall live. We made these promises trusting in God's grace, Christ's love, and the Spirit's help. We exchanged rings as symbols of our vows, and our pastor pronounced us "kin, married in the name of the Father, and of the Son, and of the Holy Spirit."

Our first act as a married couple was to serve Communion to our guests. The plates and cups we used belong to our church—our brave, beautiful, loving church. We served our pastors and elders, our home group, the friends we see every Sunday. We served our family, and we served friends visiting from out of town. At last, we served each other.

When we took our vows, we made a promise to become lifelong helpers to one another and servants to our community. The cross on the altar was also our church's, and as we stood by it, communing with our loved ones, it dawned on us that this was what it meant to be married.

Questions for Reflection

1. What traditions are important to you in a wedding? Which would you keep out of your ceremony?
2. Have you ever been to a same-sex wedding? What was the experience like for you?
3. How might same-sex weddings inform opposite-sex weddings?
4. Is marriage still relevant in today's culture? Why or why not?

An Interview with Gabriel Mudd and
Geoff Bleeker Mudd

———————— ⟨⟨∽⟩⟩ ————————

INTERFAITH AND
INTERRACIAL

Geoff Bleeker Mudd and Gabriel Mudd kept many traditions in their wedding, yet their marriage is anything but
traditional. Geoff takes issue with the accusation that by
embracing marriage as a gay man, he is mindlessly assimi-
lating into a heteronormative world. "The queerest thing
in the world," Geoff says, "is a black Christian guy and a
white Jewish guy deciding to get married and saying, 'This
is what we think marriage is.'" Geoff is Jewish and white.
When he graduated from high school, he went to college
thinking he would study to become a rabbi. His husband,
Gabriel, is black and what Geoff calls a "capital-C Christian." Gabriel grew up singing in a charismatic church and
wanted to be a Christian music star when he grew up. "But
the great glory of queerness," Geoff adds, "is getting to figure it out for yourself and deciding for yourself what you
want your marriage to be."

The differences between Gabriel and Geoff are evident
on the surface, but they also run deep. Geoff was raised
in a fairly liberal environment. He remembers attending

a gay wedding for the first time when he was fourteen or fifteen. He didn't struggle much to accept his own sexual orientation. Gabriel's family, however, is very conservative, even to this day. He didn't begin to think about his sexuality until college, and, even then, it wasn't something he allowed himself to process fully. "I had questions and issues of acceptance," he says, "but I shoved my issues with my sexuality down because I was always taught that they were wrong, sinful, bad—that you go to hell for it. As a result, my awakening to my sexuality was super delayed, because it was something I didn't want to even think about or pay attention to at all. I had an awful, unhealthy view of sex in general—not only same-sex relationships."

When Gabriel, who identifies as bisexual, finally admitted that he was attracted to men, he went directly to reparative therapy. "After I graduated from college I was weirded out because I started having feelings for both men and women," he says. "I didn't know what to do with that. I was living in New York, doing musical theater, and meeting lots of really interesting people who were challenging my worldview and pushing my boundaries. But at the same time, I was attending a conservative evangelical church and had gone into worship ministry at that church." He makes air quotes when he says he eventually talked to his pastor about his "struggles with SSA," which stands for same-sex attraction. The pastor told him that if he wanted to continue in ministry he would have to go through an ex-gay program. "I went for a couple of years, but finally, it got to the point where I grew tired of hating myself," he says. "I honestly couldn't believe that God would hate me so much that he would send me to hell for my sexuality, which I had legitimately prayed about, fasted about, and tried to change for years—hoping something would change, but nothing changed."

The church gave Gabriel an ultimatum, requiring that he either publicly renounce his orientation or leave. So he left. He needed time, he says, to go on a journey of self-discovery and meet other Christians who thought differently from the people he knew growing up. By the time he met Geoff, he had fully reconciled his love of God, and the knowledge that God loves him, with his bisexual identity, which in terms of the spectrum leans toward the same sex. He knew he wanted to date someone who would respect his faith, wouldn't put him down for it, and was open to dating people of other faiths.

Geoff ended up not becoming a rabbi, but his faith continued to inform his relationship to learning, to social justice, and to the way he sees the world. He knew he wanted to marry someone who could understand those deeper underpinnings of how we approach life. But growing up in Texas, he was wary of ultraconservative Christians and people who spoke "Christianese" as fluently as Gabriel does. "Until I met Gabriel," he says, "I didn't think I could be with someone who was as *actively* Christian as he is—meaning, someone who doesn't just have faith and sometimes goes to church but who actually wants to be in worship ministry and attend Christian conferences."

In marriage, the blending of their religions has been seamless. They attend Passover seders and Easter dinners. In December, they light a menorah alongside a Christmas tree. But beyond those outward expressions, each says his spiritual expression has been made richer by the other's presence in his life. They feel closer to God and have gained deeper understandings of the Divine.

"Seeing my Christian faith through a Jewish lens has helped me better understand our foundations," Gabriel says, "especially the way Reform Judaism sees the world— that has really opened my eyes. As Christians we are taught that we are born into sin and everything is tainted by sin—you are sinful, and we are fallen. But the Jewish belief, as I understand it, is that we're born into a world of sin—there is sin in the world, but it's not you who is sinful. This gives you a completely different outlook on both how you receive grace for yourself and how you seek to be more socially aware, to heal the world, to seek justice and help redeem the world."

Geoff has begun to understand Christianity better than he did growing up as a religious minority in the Bible Belt: "For me, the notion of grace that I've learned from Gabriel is very different from what I learned growing up. For us, we talk about grace, but very differently. We talk about the fact that we should be gracious to each other and that we should forgive one another, but this grace and forgiveness is earned. The notion of grace that is unearned, the idea of coming at something from a place of grace initially, is something I have gained."

Beyond their faith, they have also had to struggle with the challenges of being an interracial couple. "In the gay and bi communities, especially," says Gabriel, "dating a black man is something that is still fetishized, and people will use that to minimize our relationship." Geoff, who was passionate about racial justice long before he met Gabriel, now faces pushback. "People will dismiss anything I have to say, telling me I'm only saying it because my husband is black, and that is incredibly frustrating," he says. Gabriel points out that his family was wary of him marrying a white person, but their distress at him marrying a man eclipsed everything else.

Marriage has taught them not to hide—from themselves or others. "We have a ketubah—our Jewish marriage contract—on our wall, and I see that every day," Geoff says. "It reminds me of the commitment we made. It encourages me to get up and work because now I'm not alone—there is someone else who is also relying on me."

Geoff's relationship advice:
"Remember that you are only your own frame of reference. And in order to have a successful relationship, you must step out of your frame of reference and try to see things from the other's perspective."

Gabriel's relationship advice:

"You must be open and listen. There's an empathy that God gives us, and we must use this to listen to our spouse's heart. And even in disagreement, always assume positive intent."

CHAPTER 8

FORSAKING
ALL OTHERS

We have heard some married couples say that the word *divorce* isn't part of their vocabulary—they refuse to even think about it. At face value, this sentiment sounds like a strong foundation for lasting commitment, but we think it can also have unintended consequences. Pretending that divorce isn't a reality that can afflict any couple is like pretending illness and death aren't part of life. We don't fear the word *divorce*. We talk about it periodically because we never want to get to a place where we would actually consider divorcing. We want our marriage to last for the rest of our lives. Talking about divorce—understanding its causes and the ways to prevent it—is as necessary for the health of your marriage as medical screenings and good nutrition are for the health of your body.

We chose traditional Christian wedding vows when we planned our ceremony because we recognize in those promises the practices that keep divorce at bay: caring for each other, giving yourself to the other, enduring all things, and bearing all things—no matter what life brings. These

121

practices are more difficult than they sound. They require growing so close to another person that you become, as the Bible puts it, "one flesh." That kind of devotion calls for a singular focus. It requires the faithfulness of "forsaking all others for as long as you both shall live."

Of all the vows, it was this last one that gave us the most pause in the months leading up to our wedding. Neither of us was coming to our relationship as a virgin. Both of us had enough self-awareness to question our capacity for fidelity. David spent a season of life in the hook-up culture. I (Constantino) had been in a nine-year relationship that had ended with an affair. Promiscuity and infidelity forced us to ask hard questions about our ability to commit. Rather than hiding or ignoring the specters of divorce and infidelity, we keep them in front of us, in full view, where they can never catch us by surprise. But to fully see these dangers requires brutal honesty about our capacity to break commitments, and that requires an uncomfortable journey into my past.

Constantino's Three-Year Affair

My partner and I lived on 74th Street. The gym was on 76th. My lover lived on 68th. I often took the long way home, or the long way to the gym. I was in great shape, maybe, but no workout ever lasts four hours.

When the affair started, we lived on opposite sides of Manhattan. My partner, Richard, and I were in the East Village, and Charles was in Washington Heights (their names changed for privacy). Charles and I met in spring, in an elevator at the Waldorf-Astoria. We were headed to the same black-tie event. He was in a rented tux; I was wearing my own because I felt a need to own such trappings back then. Richard had stayed home, as he often preferred to do.

Charles and I didn't immediately hook up. We were drawn to each other, but nothing happened until summer, when we both found ourselves in Washington, DC, at the same time for work. Richard and I had been together for six years. We had met, started dating, and moved in together, also in DC—not too far from where Charles and I would end up in bed. The irony did not escape me.

Richard and I hadn't had sex in nearly four years. We were great friends and great partners. We cared for each other deeply. We had a dog we both loved and a New York apartment we had turned into a home. We were comfortable with each other and treated each other well. But there was no passion in our relationship; there weren't even that many fights.

Charles wasn't the first guy with whom I'd cheated. But the others were no one special—a few random hookups here and there, whenever the months of sexlessness weakened my desire to be faithful. To this day I have trouble forgiving myself. Richard caught me—or at least suspected me—a few times. But he never dumped me. And I always resolved never to do it again. I don't know if we stayed together out of love or out of fear of being alone. Maybe both. We'd met when we were twenty-two, and we'd seen each other through some difficult times—it was scary to think of what life would look like without each other. It was scary to be single. So I didn't walk, and he didn't kick me out.

Charles was different. I had introduced him and his boyfriend to Richard, and the four of us went out on a number of double dates. Richard liked Charles at first but soon began to distrust him. He started calling him, derisively, my "spare boyfriend." This was long before Charles and I even kissed. Charles wasn't the home-wrecking kind. He wanted nothing more than a long-term partner and a family. But he somehow fell for me. And that's what I suppose Richard saw before even I did: the way we talked—and the length of our phone conversations wasn't normal. It wasn't a healthy level of bonding for a partnered person to develop with someone else.

So the affair went on — Richard, pretending to be blind; Charles, pretending I'd someday have the guts to leave Richard; me, pretending I could carry on the charade forever. For three years this double life lasted; three years of Richard and me playing the part of the "perfect gay couple that has been together almost a decade"; three years of Charles getting frustrated with me, breaking up with me, and taking me back; three years of living every cliché in the book, including the work trips that were the only times Charles and I could pretend to be a normal couple.

Both relationships ended at about the same time. Charles finally got tired of me, my cowardice, and my duplicity. The shock of losing him caused me to end things with Richard. I was left with nothing. I left New York for a year. I became a vagrant of sorts — a traveling writer living off a meager stipend. When I came back, I had less than two thousand dollars in the bank, no job, no home, no dog, no boyfriend, and no partner. That tuxedo I owned? Richard threw it away, along with most of my possessions, when he moved out of the apartment we'd shared.

As far as I know, Richard hasn't forgiven me for what I did, and I don't think he ever will. I doubt he'll ever speak to me again. It has now been longer since we last saw each other than it was that we lived together. But the truth remains that I deeply mistreated Richard and Charles both. They are both good men. Both deserved better than they received from me. Both deserved to be loved by someone better than who I was.

That year away, and that return to New York with almost nothing, gave me that which I've come to cherish most: a relationship with God. During that year I learned how to pray, and I found myself for the first time in my life in communion with the Spirit. It was then that I turned to the Gospels and encountered Jesus — and fell in love with *him*.

I've never been able to explain my conversion. No one preached at me, no one taught me any prayers, no one brought me to Christ. God simply came to me, whispered to me, and taught my heart to see. And what I saw most vividly was the way in which I had hurt these two men.

My most terrible memories, which I nonetheless treasure, are from the time that followed my breakups. I remember a stretch of days, possibly a week, when I could not stop crying. I held up at work, at church, and whenever I was with someone. But a switch flipped the moment I was alone, and a rush of shameful, lonely tears unlike any I've known before or since would overcome me. I felt a deep pain that was physical, and real, yet somehow not of my body. I later tried to describe the feeling to my pastor. "It's like God was washing my soul," I said. "But with a *Brillo pad.*"

I shared all of this with David before we even started dating. I told him all about Richard and Charles. He has now read through all my letters and has even helped me destroy those I decided were no longer worth keeping. He knows it all. He has even met Charles—who is himself married now. David knows me fully, and more deeply than either of my exes ever did.

I love David with a passion and depth I'd never known before. I've chosen him, and I've given myself to him with a conviction I didn't think possible for me. And his love has healed me. God has used him as a balm to soothe the rawness left by that Brillo pad. David's grace toward me has mirrored that which I've come to know from Christ.

Sometimes at night when I have trouble sleeping, I sit in the living room and question myself, wondering if I'm fundamentally bad, if the adage that "once a cheater, always a cheater" is true. But then I walk into our bedroom and hear him breathing, with a faint strand of moonlight kissing his face—and my heart blooms. The Holy Spirit, who is the very essence of love, fills me and reminds me that my vow is strong, that my vow is sacred, that my vow is forgiveness itself—and for that reason, I know it will always be kept.

An Encounter with an Ex

I (David) hadn't been in a long-term relationship prior to meeting Constantino, but during my single years—both in and out of the closet, in and out of reparative therapy—I too had sexual liaisons with others. Like Constantino, I questioned my ability to commit to one man. Sex had always been an unhealthy outlet for me, a conduit of shame, and a way to numb the pain of facing who I really was. What we realized during our early conversations about fidelity and marriage was that both of us feared the past versions of ourselves—the weaker young men we had been.

We feared our baggage. But marriage, whether we like it or not, brings about a slow unpacking of this baggage. And sometimes what we pull out of our old suitcases is a person—namely, an ex. Whenever exes surface from the storage trunks of our past, there's the question of what to do with them. Should we stuff them back down, buried forever under the mothballs of other memories? Or should we pull them out for our spouse to see, an out-of-date fashion that's a reminder of a particular time in life?

Facing the ghosts of our past isn't pleasant, but it is the only way to rid them of their power to loom over our future. So when we had an opportunity during our first year of marriage to look in the eye the ghost we feared most—Constantino's infidelity—we took it. We went to go meet Constantino's ex together.

Visiting New York was a chance for Constantino to relive his formative years and reconnect with the people and places that were meaningful to him. For me, it was an opportunity to experience my husband's history through tangible people and places rather than through the second-hand accounts of his own storytelling. Part of that history involved his past relationship and the affair that ended it, and we struggled with whether to invite that part of his past into our present.

I knew that prior to meeting me, Constantino had reconnected with Charles. They no longer had any feelings for each other, but they also didn't feel animosity. They'd occasionally kept in touch—an email once a year or so. When Constantino asked if I wanted to meet him while we were in New York, my initial response was swift and decisive: *No.* I wasn't threatened by meeting him, and it wasn't that I was afraid for our marriage—Charles is also happily married, and he and his husband had recently become fathers. My resistance was more about whether I was prepared to make Constantino's former relationships—particularly his three-year affair—more real by meeting the guy who had played the part of "the other man" in their drama. I wondered whether it would be healthier to simply keep that relationship relegated to Constantino's memories. I felt as if we might be dredging up the past for no good reason.

After thinking about it for a day, though, I changed my mind. Shakespeare concisely describes my reasoning: "What's past is prologue." Our present is built upon the foundation of a past that has, in essence, set the stage for our current lives. Our wounds, our values, our character—all of these are a product of the lives we have lived. In choosing to marry Constantino, I have chosen to go deep with this one person in my life, and part of going deep is working to understand as much about him as I can. By knowing the people who were once meaningful to him, I can get a better sense of who he was and where he came from.

So we met. And it was fine. Charles was at home watching his son while his husband and mother-in-law were out. It was late morning, and Charles made us guacamole and mimosas. We chatted about New York, parenthood, and our jobs. Constantino got a chance to watch his ex be a father. I had the opportunity to put a face and a personality to someone who once held a place of importance in Constantino's life. The meeting was pleasant and relaxed, and Charles appeared to me as simply another background detail in the mural of my husband's past. It was mostly anticlimactic; the ways in which I had built up Constantino's exes in my mind quickly deflated. When we parted ways after an hour or so, I was glad we had gotten together. I felt as if our meeting helped me peel away another translucent layer of my husband's past, allowing me to see him a little bit more clearly. It brought closure for both of us, and it disarmed the specter of infidelity that we had feared. I realized later that meeting Constantino's ex wasn't about meeting another person, but about meeting a new facet of Constantino himself. In an effort to be vulnerable and known, my husband invited me into his period of deepest shame, and I love him all the more for it.

Flirtations, Past and Present

One thing we did right in our approach to this encounter is that, when it came to meeting Charles, Constantino followed my lead. He allowed me to be the decision maker over whether we met and what that encounter would look like. Constantino would, if I asked it of him, never see or communicate with his ex again. More broadly, we've made a habit of sharing honestly and openly about our pasts, the good relationships and the bad. It's this kind of vulnerability that has built the trust we need to not be threatened by each other's exes. As part of that trust, we've set boundaries. Neither of us would, for example, meet with an ex without first asking permission from the other. If one of us hears from an ex, or for any reason reaches out to an ex, he shares that with the other.

This doesn't mean that every ex is a healthy person to allow into your lives. Some couples might find in the suitcases of their past casual flings, unhealthy relationships, or partners one of them never fully got over. Those kinds of exes deserve to be buried forever in the bottom of your baggage. It doesn't mean you never talk about them or share the ways in which the relationship shaped you; it simply means that the person would not be an edifying addition to your current life and marriage.

We've learned that it's important to let your spouse have the final say in whether an ex occupies any space in your shared present. Your priority is to keep up the health of your marriage, not to maintain the relationships of your past. Sometimes that means honoring a request from your spouse that seems unreasonable. Your wife may want you to delete phone numbers and unfriend exes on Facebook, even if you haven't talked to them in ages. Your husband might even have to cut ties with a partner-turned-friend with whom you're close. An action that severe may point to deeper trust issues in your marriage that you need to work through, but we ultimately believe in spousal prerogative in these circumstances.

We all hope to find that one partner who's the right fit for us. Once we do, should we forever lock the trunk of the ill-fitting exes of our past? Not necessarily. A careful, cautious search through each other's baggage is sometimes the best way to understand the prologue to your shared story.

Constantino's past is one of the reasons we talk so openly about divorce and about our desire to nurture our relationship consistently so that we never go down that route. It is, after all, a route Constantino is familiar with. He and Richard were not married, because that wasn't an option for them back then, but their breakup was very much like a divorce. They co-owned most of their possessions, and their finances were combined. They even had to fight over the custody of their dog; Richard kept him, and Constantino's heart still aches for his lost pooch. When we look at the way things transpired in his previous relationships, it is evident that a lack of intentionality is what led to their demise.

The friendship he developed with Charles early on was problematic. Had he thought of forsaking others for Richard, he would not have allowed that relationship with

Charles to develop in the way it did. He wouldn't have spent hours on the phone with Charles, he wouldn't have texted Charles throughout the day, he wouldn't have gone out for drinks or dinner with Charles without their respective boyfriends. If he had taken a vow, and thought of it seriously, he would not have pushed against it the way he pushed against the promise he'd made Richard to be exclusive and faithful.

Marriage vows are meant to be stronger than the promises of dating. We take ours seriously because we can easily see in our own pasts what their absence can do to a relationship. But that doesn't mean others always do. We both wear wedding rings, and we write about marriage. It should be obvious to anyone who meets us, either online or in real life, that we are off the market. Yet we've both faced interactions that show not everyone believes our marital status has rendered us unavailable.

Constantino was greeted once with "What's up, stud?" by someone on Facebook who had previously asked another one of our married friends what his boundaries "actually" were. But this isn't about us specifically. These kinds of advances are so frequent among our group of married and partnered gay friends that it is not unusual for one of us to share with the others a tale of an egregious interaction (and often ones more explicit than "What's up, stud?").

Is this a reinterpretation of marriage, or something else? Our sense is that some gay men have not had the practical experience of having to respect nuptial boundaries. Straight men and women have long encountered married people they might be attracted to and have discovered how to interact with them appropriately. Enticing a married person is taboo in most cultures — in faith-based communities for sure, but even the broader secular culture frowns upon this indiscretion. That's certainly not to say all straight people abide by these rules, but most would generally agree that these boundaries exist.

Same-sex marriage is relatively new, on the other hand, and so those boundaries are poorly defined. For most of history, dating was the highest level of commitment LGBTQ people could make. Without the finality of marriage, some may have an ingrained mentality that no one is ever permanently "off the market." Because of that, and perhaps in part because some queer folks reject anything and everything that might smell of heteronormativity, there's an excessive tolerance in the LGBTQ community for sexual or romantic advances. Some gay men may disregard boundaries because, historically, there haven't been many. The secular LGBTQ community has been more comfortable with the idea of "open" relationships, and that mentality may seep into the concept of marriage, even in the Christian community.

Our interest is not in disputing or condemning open relationships and other nontraditional forms of romance, but rather looking at how these attitudes can foster a challenging environment for those who wish to make a vow before God to take one person as their spouse at the exclusion of all others.

To be clear, we are not saying that LGBTQ people are somehow more deviant than straight people; some of us simply haven't had to confront our desires as they relate to someone else's marriage. There was never a danger of a gay man making a pass at a married woman, and although we might have been attracted to a straight married man, futility kept us from flirting with him in earnest. Now gay men find themselves in a world where they're meeting married men whom they find attractive and, perhaps for the first time, a married man could be openly attracted to them as well. It's a whole new ball game.

We've received pushback on the idea that some in the LGBTQ community haven't learned respectful boundaries, and we welcome dissent; however, we've experienced and witnessed these interactions frequently enough that we felt it was appropriate to include in a book on marriage.

For those of you seeking a monogamous relationship, it's worth being aware that these dynamics exist, especially if you hang out in wider LGBTQ circles. As married people, we are ultimately responsible for setting boundaries in interacting with others. That is why we are both blunt in rejecting advances. But our hope is that those in the LGBTQ community who lack awareness about marital boundaries will come to appreciate and support fidelity for those who choose it. Save the "What's up, stud?" for the dating apps—and maybe work on your pickup lines a little.

Ultimately, marriages are most secure when spouses are committed to intentionality based on self-awareness. Acknowledge and celebrate the strengths of your marriage, but also look honestly at your weaknesses. Know what aspects of yourself could set your relationship off course. Famed psychoanalyst Carl Jung wrote frequently of the shadow self, the typically unconscious parts of ourselves that contain the least desirable aspects of our personalities: "Everyone carries a shadow, and the less it is embodied in the individual's conscious life, the blacker and denser it is."[1] Part of intentional self-awareness includes looking at our pasts and the parts of ourselves that have the potential to drive our relationships toward divorce. For us, it is looking at our past relationships and understanding how we failed at them. For you, it may be something different. Keeping your shadow in front of you is the best way to ensure it doesn't sneak up on you from behind.

Questions for Reflection

1. Is it better to talk about divorce as a possibility, or to refuse to entertain it as an option? What are the benefits and drawbacks of each approach?
2. What are your thoughts on infidelity—does it automatically doom a marriage, or is there space for redemption?
3. Do you see potential in yourself for infidelity? What is that part of you?

4. How in your relationship do you approach each other's exes? Is there space for friendship, or should they be cut out of your lives? What ground rules have you agreed upon?

5. Have you experienced flirting from others even if they know you are dating or married? How have you handled it? Have you found it to be true that the LGBTQ community especially struggles with how to respect marital boundaries, or do you think this is equally problematic for straight people?

CHAPTER 9

———— ⌘ ————

WHO'S THE WIFE?

When you're a married gay couple, you inevitably encounter a few seemingly innocuous questions from straight people: *Which one of you walked down the aisle at your wedding? Who took the other's last name? Who will stay home if you ever have kids?*

They are, in essence, all variations of the same question: *Who's the wife?*

Lest you think no one would be so bold as to utter those actual words, we have friends who have been asked that very question. It's impossible for a gay male couple to answer "Who's the wife?" or for a lesbian couple to answer "Who's the husband?" because they are fundamentally flawed questions, based on wrong assumptions that attempt to force a same-sex relationship into a heterosexual mold that is, in itself, problematic. So rather than try to answer it, questions like these become good opportunities to discuss gender roles, gender complementarity, and the ways in which all marriages, gay and straight, can step away from social rules and expectations based solely on gender.

One of the primary reasons many Christians object to same-sex relationships is that they say it defies gender complementarity. This is the idea that God made male and female uniquely different and also uniquely complemented to each other. While it is true that there are differences between male and female, the conclusions that have been extrapolated from that observation have caused endless abuses and oppression, probably more so for heterosexual women in the span of history than for LGBTQ people. This idea of complementarity in marriage manifests itself as hierarchy, the idea that the man leads as the head of a household and the woman follows and supports.

So when two men or two women decide to marry, many Christians attempt to place the couple into gender roles because they can't understand any other paradigm. In the minds of critics and those who don't understand, there must be a "man" role and a "woman" role, even if actual genders don't align. Hence the question: *Who's the wife?* The prospect of deconstructing that entire tradition is simply too much for some people to wrap their heads around. But just because the nature of same-sex relationships may be difficult to digest doesn't mean we should automatically disregard them. Many of Jesus' parables were difficult to understand; being challenged by an idea is not an excuse to dismiss it, but rather an opportunity to reexamine our understanding of God and the nature of God's love.

Part of what we love most about being in a same-sex relationship is that those gender roles don't apply any-more. Neither of us is expected to be the breadwinner, or the primary childcare provider, or the one who has the last say during a disagreement. Instead, we each get to use our God-given skills and proclivities to build a functional, highly customized relationship that works best for us. Constantino hates financials, so I pay most of the bills. I'm worse at keeping up relationships, so Constantino manages our calendar and schedules social events. We've taken turns as the majority breadwinner.

All couples, gay and straight alike, should have the freedom to dismantle the gender roles to which they have been assigned. While tradition places men and women in clearly defined positions within the family, there is no biblical foundation for it. When we read Paul's letters about a woman's place in the family and the church, we must read beyond the literal commandments and ask ourselves what the context is for that culture and situation. We should seek to discern what theologian James Brownson calls the "moral logic" behind Paul's words.[1] That is to say, what are Paul's words getting at? What is he trying to say about how we should live? When he tells women they must cover their heads and avoid speaking in church, is he addressing an issue in that time and culture, or is he giving a blanket command in perpetuity? If you are a woman (or married to a woman) who doesn't wear a head covering, then you must believe that the commands found in the Bible can have both a literal directive and a broader application. Paul may have been instructing women to be silent in church not because there was anything wrong with it from a theological perspective, but because in that particular context it was distracting people from hearing the message of the gospel. And if that is true, must we not at least be open to the idea that other commands in the Bible have an underlying universal truth that manifests itself differently throughout history? It's possible to read the Bible faithfully without reading it literally.

Dismantling gender roles does not in the slightest way diminish the call for mutual submission and sacrifice. There is still inherent in the relationship the same giving over of oneself that characterizes a God-centered marriage.

So if someone asks us, "Who's the wife?" the quick answer is "Neither of us." We both fulfill unique roles that defy gender-assigned norms. We both perform "husband" duties, and we both perform "wife" duties, knowing that these gendered characterizations are arbitrary. And there's nothing shameful about any of it. We accomplish the same

thing all marriages do, but we do it in our own way—
customized just for us.

The best part about being in a same-sex marriage is that
it is naturally egalitarian. Since neither one of us is "the wife"
and both of us are "the husband," we simply get to be David
and Constantino—two individuals with equally valid opinions and input. Gender never plays a role in our dynamic.

Accepting Each Other's Influence

As gay husbands, it seems we are naturally adept at something many straight husbands struggle with: accepting
influence from our spouse. In a long-term study of 130 heterosexual couples, men who allowed their wives to influence them had happier relationships and were less likely
to eventually divorce than men who resisted their wives'
influence.[2] Statistically speaking, when a man refuses to
share power with his partner, there is an 81 percent chance
that his marriage will self-destruct.

Back when we were engaged, we had a supportive
friend from church ask earnestly which one of us would
make the "final decisions." We shared a confused look,
prompting her to explain that even though she and her
husband have a largely egalitarian marriage, it is he who
has the final say when they disagree. This, she told us, was
something they explicitly determined years ago during
premarital counseling.

This notion that "father knows best" may seem anti-
quated, but whether we admit it or not, it is still deeply
ingrained in our culture. Some men, especially those in conservative or evangelical circles, have difficulty letting go of
the idea that their opinions are ultimately the only ones
that matter. Ironically, the ones who learn to yield—who
convey genuine respect for their spouses' opinions—are
the ones with the happiest marriages. These men are what
the Gottman Institute, the world's leading organization for

the research-based study of marriage and relationships, calls emotionally intelligent husbands.[3]

Letting your partner influence you is especially important when it comes to conflict resolution. All couples argue—because everyone faces moments of anger, frustration, and other negative emotions—but couples who reduce negativity by deploying repair attempts (see chapter 10) have stronger marriages. Research also shows that 65 percent of men respond to conflict by escalating the negativity rather than helping to diffuse it. None of this is to say that women can't be stubborn too, but the data appears to indicate that men find it harder to let their guard down and yield.

Being gay hasn't made us immune to that tendency. We can both be as hardheaded as the next guy, and we don't like admitting when we're wrong. The difference in our marriage is that culture hasn't trained us to automatically assume that our spouse will eventually have to yield. If one of us wants to be stubborn, he better be prepared to justify it by voicing the reasons why he feels so strongly about whatever it is we're discussing. And by the same token, we had both better be willing to listen.

A twelve-year study of committed same-sex couples found that they are less likely than straight couples to use hostile emotional tactics—including domineering, belligerence, and fear—with each other.[4] It suggests that fairness and power sharing between partners is more ingrained in gay and lesbian relationships than in straight ones. (See our interview with Dr. Julie Schwartz Gottman for more on this.)

Learning how to yield not only makes your relationship stronger, but it makes you grow as a person. Marriage has taught us to be better friends, better listeners to others, and more open to considering opinions other than our own. Accepting your spouse's influence may not always come naturally, but the growth you derive from that emotional intelligence leads to healthier relationships not only at home but in every realm of life.

A Queer Decision on Last Names

I (Constantino) offered one of the biggest yields in our relationship before we even got married. I offered to change my last name.

For most of my life, my identity has resided in my name. I was born into a family that prides itself in its genealogy, and I can easily trace my ancestors back to the 1500s. I could go further if I did some research. I belong to the sixth generation of Diaz-Durans, a hyphenated surname that resulted from the union in the nineteenth century of two once-powerful Spanish houses in Central America. I count some remarkable men and women among my ancestors, and I was raised to pay reverence to my last name. But ultimately I decided to abandon it for something more important.

The process of unifying in marriage usually results in a name change for one of the spouses, but rarely, at least in opposite-sex marriages, is it ever a husband. I don't want to minimize the feelings of women who have given up their maiden names upon marriage, but they grow up knowing it's a possibility, and many even look forward to it. As a man, you never think your name is going to change. The very fact that we have the expression "maiden name" but not "bachelor name" is telling. At play are notions of gender roles, submission, and even ownership. In Spanish tradition, married women not only take their husband's name, but they add the preposition *de*, meaning "property of," before it. I was all too aware that the decision I made to become Constantino Khalaf would make me, in some people's eyes, the "wife."

David and I decided to share a name because we think it brings cohesion to a family unit. We like the message it conveys, the kinship it fosters, and the sense of belonging it gives us. David is now my immediate family, and I am his; it made sense for our last name to be the same. We like being "the Khalafs." If we choose to have children, we'd want them to share their last name with both of us. We would want there to be no question that we are both their parents — that they belong to both of us, and we both belong to them.

That we would share a name was settled without much question, but my taking David's wasn't a given. We had many conversations about it in which we considered the various alternatives. We joked about combining "Khalaf" and "Duran" to get Khan, and then naming our daughter Chaka. We even talked about both changing our surnames to something new.

The choices around the last name are as varied as the married same-sex couples we know. Some have hyphenated, some have taken one of the spouse's names, and some have created entirely new names. A gay couple we know read from Acts 8 at their wedding, explaining that they admire Philip's welcoming heart and his decision to baptize the Ethiopian eunuch. They then announced that they were changing their last names to Phillips (a name that wasn't found in either of their families) because they want their marriage to emulate that saint's love for those who are different and his passion for sharing the gospel. There are also couples in which both spouses choose to keep their family names. The surname decision is perhaps the most visible display of egalitarianism in same-sex marriages. Like so many issues in LGBTQ relationships, there is not a predetermined solution; the decision requires thoughtfulness, intentionality, and mutual agreement. Couples must choose what's right for them.

One of the reasons why I offered to change my name was that I've been slowly shedding names since I was born. My parents' intended name for me was Constantino, after my dad's grandfather, but they also named me Arturo, after my mom's dad. My mom loved her father, but no one ever actually called me by his name, so though it appears on my birth certificate, it has never registered in my consciousness. In the Spanish tradition, my mother's maiden name was also part of my legal name growing up. Since my dad's last name was hyphenated, it meant I essentially had three surnames: Diaz-Duran Alvarado. When I moved permanently to the United States, my father's last name became my only legal name, and I embraced the opportunity to go by something shorter.

Constantino Diaz-Duran is the name by which everyone who met me before 2013 knew me. I made the decision to drop the "Diaz" and the hyphen for the sake of minimizing and simplifying. It happened during a year I spent walking across the country with nothing but what I could fit in a backpack; the road taught me the virtues of carrying as little as possible. So when the time came for us to have a more serious conversation about names, I realized that the transition would be easier for me. I had unintentionally prepared myself for it.

Becoming Constantino Khalaf does not make me any less a scion of the family that bred me. I will continue to honor my father and grandfather, the great-grandfather whose given name I share, and my forefathers before him. Changing my last name is not a rejection of my father or his family's history any more than dropping *Alvarado* was a rejection of my mother or her family. If David and I have children, I will teach them this history, and I will share with them the stories my grandfather shared with me. I will share with them my memories and what has made me who I am, because I would never want to be a stranger to them.

Changing my name doesn't make me a new person, and it is not a disavowal of my past. It is more about cleaving than it is about leaving. It's about sharing a name with my next of kin—my husband, and perhaps someday my children—even if it means no longer sharing one with my parents and grandparents. I decided at the last minute when we got our marriage license to keep Diaz-Duran as my middle name. I don't use it socially or professionally, but I'm glad it still appears on my passport. More than on paper, however, I'll always carry Diaz-Duran in my blood, in my heart, and in the dreams I still have of sitting with my late beloved grandpa just one more time.

Learning Dependence

We've found that yielding and accepting influence are crucial components in disrupting gender norms and facilitating an egalitarian marriage. These habits result from a posture of humility, a willingness to surrender power and defer to another person. But marriage isn't only about giving in; it's also giving *of*. It's a surrender not only of power but of self. That's why we've found it so important not only to yield to each other but to practice turning to each other as a secure base.

In their book *Attached*, Amir Levine and Rachel S. F. Heller describe a "secure base" as someone who we believe is wholly protective and supportive of us. Such a person is one with whom we are completely vulnerable because we believe their love for us is unconditional and immutable. *Secure base* was first used in attachment theory in the field of relational psychology, and it asserts that our approaches to connection are developed early in life.[5] Typically the term is used to describe the relationship between a young child and a parent, but Levine and Heller apply attachment theory to romantic relationships. If we have a secure base, they write, "the world is at our feet. We can take risks, be creative, and pursue our dreams. And if we lack that sense of security . . . we'll find it much harder to focus and engage in life."[6]

But what if we have trouble making our spouse our secure base? What if we're not used to being completely vulnerable, or we're poorly adjusted to being reliant on another? Although this can happen with any person, men may have more trouble making this shift because they have traditionally held the family roles of leader and provider. In the same way men may be poorly equipped to yield power, they may also struggle with turning to their spouses as emotional anchors.

In our relationship, Constantino has no problem making me his secure base because he tends slightly toward what's called an "anxious" attachment style, meaning he craves intimacy but can become preoccupied with the stability of a relationship and the other person's ability to love him back. And because he has a limited relationship with his parents due to their rejection of his sexuality, he spent years feeling unanchored and without security. When our relationship grew serious, it was easy and natural for him to turn to me for support.

I, however, tend toward what's called an "avoidant" attachment style, meaning I understand intimacy to be a threat to independence, and so I tend to thwart relationships that become too close. My most-used phrase as a child was "I'll do it myself!" Despite this tendency toward independence, I have always had an extremely secure relationship with my parents. I'm used to turning to them whenever I have a problem or need advice.

The combination of my independence and the deeply established secure base in my parents means that I rarely turn to others for support. That was fine while I was single, but in marriage it has made Constantino feel unwanted and unneeded.

When we were buying our first home together, we sought out experts and family for advice, but Constantino always turned to me to discuss issues and express feelings of excitement or fear. Conversely, I tried to handle problems on my own and, when I couldn't, turned to my parents or real estate experts to figure things out. The result was that Constantino felt left out of the process. Rather than being at the helm of the ship with me, he felt as if he were relegated to swabbing the decks.

My failure to turn toward my husband as my secure base made him feel useless. After all, if I display no outward need for Constantino, what assurance does he have about the future of the relationship? This triggered the anxious attachment style he exhibits when he doesn't feel secure in a relationship. Combine that with my avoidant style and it became a recipe for conflict.

I have never had a problem yielding to Constantino and accepting his influence, but I struggle with relying on Constantino, especially in sharing emotional burdens. We've come to understand that making your spouse your anchor is a fundamental element of kinship. First, it requires vulnerability. Relationships are always stronger when we feel as if we both fully see the other and are fully seen ourselves. That's the essence of intimacy. Second, it fosters mutual dependence. That may sound distasteful in a culture that celebrates independence, but a mutual needing of each other is what strengthens a marriage's commitment and security. It creates a relationship that functions like a team, with an us-against-the-world kind of camaraderie.

In fact, Levine and Heller state that healthy dependence can actually foster independence: "The ability to step into the world on our own often stems from the knowledge that there is someone beside us whom we can count on—this is the 'dependency paradox' . . . If you want to take the road to independence and happiness, find the right person to depend on and travel down it with that person."[7]

To do that, some of us must first learn dependence. Others may have to relearn dependence in ways that are healthy rather than in ways that foster fear and anxiety. If we can learn to attach in deep and healthy ways, many of the relational problems that plague marriages will slip away.

Yielding, influencing, and depending. Not only does this feel like a healthier, more effective way to do relationship than the complementarian model of marriage based on gender roles, but it feels to us more like the dynamic of the Holy Trinity. It's a mutual giving of self and a consistent turning toward one another in an endless circle of love. Perhaps modern kinship is more like ancient kinship. Perhaps it is what kinship was always meant to be.

Questions for Reflection

1. Have you gotten any "Who's the wife? Who's the husband?" questions directed toward your relationship? What were they, and how did you respond?
2. What do you say to people who use gender complementarity as the basis for their opposition to same-sex marriage?
3. Have you talked about some of the bigger questions about your relationship, such as changing last names? If you've reached a decision, how did you come by it? Are there other big decisions you're struggling with?
4. In what ways do you yield and accept influence from your partner? In what ways do you resist?
5. Do you view your partner as a "secure base"? Why or why not?

⧟

A NONQUEER
PERSPECTIVE

LGBTQ couples aren't the only ones feeling as if the church's traditional teachings on marriage ignore reality. "Most people, even when they say they're complementarian, function in a more egalitarian way," says Christian author Rachel Held Evans. "Almost every marriage I have witnessed gets to a point where you just can't keep to these strict traditional gender roles." This break with gender roles is sometimes forced by unwanted circumstances, such as a husband getting laid off and the wife becoming the sole provider of income. But most of the time it's simply because the spouses recognize that partnership in marriage works better than hierarchy. "From my parents to the people around me," says Rachel, "the marriages I've observed work like just two people trying to get along and help each other along the way."

Rachel and her husband, Dan, were both young when they got married. They were immersed in the evangelical subculture, and much of the advice they received was at odds with what they knew about themselves. "A lot of the messages we got were about how men are this way, and women are that way—so if you want to please your husband you do this, this, and this, and if you want to please your wife you do this, this, and this." They were told that men wanted respect, while women just wanted love. They were told what gifts to get for each other based on what women are supposed to like and what men are supposed to enjoy.

"It became pretty clear very early on that we didn't fit those stereotypes," Rachel says. "Nobody does. So what we found was that it's much better just to get to know the person themselves, and their personality. For instance, for our ten-year anniversary, we went to an Alabama football game, and it was exactly what I wanted. If he had been following all the rules of what women are supposed to want, I wouldn't have gotten that gift."

Beyond stereotypes around what women want, perhaps the more pernicious messages they received were surrounding topics of submission and control. "Those were messages that we had to set aside in order to make our marriage work," Rachel says. "And it wasn't like we sat down one day and said, 'Complementarianism does not fit our lifestyle!' It just naturally happened that we became partners. One person wasn't always making more money than the other person; one person wasn't doing all the housework. Instead, we settled into roles based on what we were good at. But that was definitely going against some expectations that were placed upon us, and it took a little while to shake those expectations off."

Still, the pressure is such in some Christian circles that even couples who can't make complementarianism work feel compelled to at least pretend that they abide by it. "In more negative situations," Rachel says, "they try to force it. And when it doesn't work, it leads to heartache and disappointment, and unfulfilled expectations—all the things that can wreck a marriage."

The problem, Rachel says, is that Christian couples often have too much invested in complementarianism to really question it. "People make very important life decisions based on that model for marriage. So if ten or fifteen years down the road that framework gets questioned, they have too much emotionally invested to seriously consider changing their minds. It's a sunk-cost fallacy, but I think we all have trouble when our worldview gets challenged and we start thinking about choices we would have made differently if we'd known there were other options."

One of Rachel's books, *A Year of Biblical Womanhood*, chronicles a year she spent abiding by the rules presumably set out for women in Scripture. She wanted to prove that no one really lives that way and thus to stop Christians from using that term to force women into submission. The experience led her to rethink the household codes set out in the New Testament — the passages used by conservative men to keep women relegated to the kitchen.

"I began to notice," she explains, "that every single instance in which Scripture instructs wives to submit to their husbands is either preceded or followed by instructions for slaves to obey their masters. And this should make us question whether this is really about reinforcing the Greco-Roman household structure, or if it's talking about imitating Christ within that very imperfect model. The big questions we should be asking are these: 'Is this teaching us the ideal structure for the household? Does God's dream for the household include wives who submit to their husband and slaves who obey their masters?' Or is it simply telling us that it is possible to imitate Christ even within a patriarchal and oppressive culture?"

Shedding her conservative evangelical beliefs about gender roles and marriage eventually led Rachel to befriend and affirm same-sex couples. Now that she's a mother, she's grateful to have LGBTQ friends who can act as role models for her children, whether they grow up to be part of the LGBTQ community or not. "It's a real gift to be able to have my kids grow up surrounded by families and relationships that don't look just like their mom and dad," she says, "because not every relationship is going to look like their mom and dad, and that's a good thing for them to know at a young age."

Beyond that, she values the lessons that everyone can learn from LGBTQ people who choose to press into both relationship and faith: "These are people whose faith and marriages have been hard won, people who choose to do these things out of health and wholeness and happiness, even when their family disapproves or their church disapproves. That's a great model for me, encouraging me to also choose health and wholeness even when it's hard. The same-sex couples in my life have taught me that living in truth is so worth it even when it is extremely difficult."

"In terms of marriage," she adds, LGBTQ couples "are a great example to all of us that you don't have to fit into ancient stereotypes or have some sort of hierarchy to have a relationship that is glorifying to God—a union that is sacramental in nature, that's mutually giving and mutually respectful, even mutually submissive and deferential. They are a testimony to the fact that marriage isn't about people falling into roles, but rather about sacrifice, love, and commitment."

Rachel's relationship advice:
"Keep your sense of humor, and make each other laugh. Try to always maintain that throughout the good and bad stages of life. Because when things have really gone down the drain, it's that shared sense of humor and the ability to laugh at the situation together that will get you through."

CHAPTER 10

─────── ⚭ ───────

ON THE OTHER SIDE
OF VOWS

If you're reading this book, you're most likely married, headed toward marriage, or hope to one day be so. Many of us who are LGBTQ place great hope and expectation in marriage because we grew up in a world where it wasn't a prospect for us. The road that once looked so bleak is now brimming with possibility. It's easy, then, to see a wedding as a finish line rather than the mile marker that it is. So much effort has gone into making each LGBTQ marriage a reality, both at a cultural level for the community and at a personal level for the couple, that we might neglect to look at what's on the other side of our nuptials.

Same-sex marriage is still relatively novel, especially among faith communities. Once we cross that mile marker, what does gay marriage actually look like? What does trans marriage look like? Or bi marriage? Although there have been legal same-sex domestic partnerships and civil unions for decades, the federal recognition of same-sex marriage in 2015 means that most marriages are still relatively young.

It will be decades before we see an abundance of same-sex spouses who have been legally married forty or fifty years.

Critics have had their own ideas of what same-sex marriage would look like. Long before the *Obergefell* ruling, conservative writer Stanley Kurtz wrote in the neoconservative magazine *Commentary* that the "proudly promiscuous" LGBTQ population may not even want marriage: "To suppose that legally conferring the word 'marriage' on the union of two gay men will somehow magically domesticate them both is to indulge in fantasy. . . . Homosexuality, and particularly male homosexuality, is by its very nature incompatible with the norms of traditional monogamous marriage."[1]

Kurtz seemed to think so little of gay men and women that he believed us to be incapable of fidelity, commitment, and domesticity. We were, according to Kurtz, a fundamentally deviant population destined to upend and ultimately destroy the institution of marriage.

We can't speak for the domestic life of every married same-sex couple, but we can pull back the veil on our own. For us, once the stress and excitement of the wedding had passed, and after the novelty of being married and using the word *husband* had worn off, what was left felt, for lack of a better word, normal. As we settled into the daily rhythms of marriage, the issues we've faced are not ones borne of existential crises over sexuality. They have nothing to do with conflicts resulting from an "imbalanced" marriage of two men or our fundamentally promiscuous nature. Rather, our conflicts almost always stem from the mundane—the typical issues every couple faces in doing life together. It has been refreshing to discover how, in many ways, our marriage is conventional and rather ordinary.

Our anecdotal discovery supports the findings of research on same-sex couples. According to a study conducted by the Gottman Institute, relationship satisfaction and quality for same-sex couples are about the same as for straight couples, and conflicts for gay couples are most likely to arise from the everyday ups and downs of life.[2]

Early marriage came with all sorts of adjustments for us, from the relational to the practical. Most of the conflicts in our first couple of years stemmed from one of three problems: having mismatched expectations, struggling with the balance between intimacy and independence, and trying to "fix" the other person. We've learned that conflicts not only are OK but are a healthy part of relationship so long as we fight in constructive ways and make earnest efforts to repair our relationship afterward.

Same House, Different Blueprints

We have fond memories of the premarital counseling sessions our pastor offered us in the months leading up to our wedding. We spent many afternoons in his backyard shed, which had been converted into a cozy office lined with bookshelves, talking about our reasons for wanting to get married and our plans for the future. When we reached the topic of sex, our straight pastor didn't bat an eye in delving into discussions of male-male intimacy (though we were both blushing furiously).

There was one lasting piece of advice our pastor impressed upon us. He said the bulk of daily conflicts in marriage arise when we have differing expectations that we fail to communicate to each other. This applies to virtually everything: to something as simple as a night out, or something as important as the way in which a couple raises their children.

Our expectations are like little blueprints in our minds of how we plan on something going. If we're working from different blueprints, one of us can be working head-down on his Victorian home only to look up and see that the other is building a midcentury modern. If we get too far in the building process before realizing our error, it will be too late.

Less than a year into our marriage, when David started working in an office and I (Constantino) was working from home, we had ongoing tension the moment David got home from work. This daily reunion should have been a joyous moment of connection, but instead we found ourselves disconnected and sometimes bickering. The problem was mismatched expectations. I, having been alone and isolated all day, was eager to talk, engage, and connect. So as soon as David got home, I unleashed a flood of thoughts and feelings, including everything from crises at my work to the latest incident of the tantrum-prone boy living across the street. Talking is one of the ways I connect.

David, however, needed time to decompress after a long day at work. As an introvert and internal processor, he needs to center himself internally before he can be present for someone externally. To him, that looked like changing from his work clothes into sweats, pouring a glass of wine, and reading a book in silence for half an hour.

When I tried to love David by verbally connecting with him, David felt assaulted by the words rather than engaged by them. David would then tersely end the conversation so that he could have some time with his thoughts. I, in turn, would feel rejected, and a rift would form between us. Some nights we would talk about hurt feelings but never really identify the problem. Other nights we would attempt to move past the encounter and ignore the subtle cracks keeping us from genuine connection.

The problem was that our expectations were different for what would happen each night when David returned home. As obvious a problem as it was, it took some time for us to discover what was going on. Part of it was that David was afraid to express his need for alone time because he thought I would interpret it as rejection. Finally, David expressed that although he was happy to see me when he got home from work, what he really needed was thirty minutes of silence and personal time before we began the process of connecting. I was not hurt by the request; rather, I was happy to understand David and his needs better. From that point on, we've greeted each other warmly after a day of work, but then I hold back until David is ready to talk. After a few minutes of reading or listening to the news, David feels refreshed and can be more present for me.

Mismatched expectations have entered nearly every aspect of our relationship. One summer, David was running a two-hundred-mile relay race with some of our friends, and I was helping out by serving as the team driver. I had a vision of being a support to David: bringing him water, massaging his cramped legs, offering encouragement. But David had no expectation of such help. Self-sufficient to a flaw, David only asks for help when he has lost the capacity to do something himself (e.g., broken, bleeding, dead). We never talked in advance about our visions for the weekend, and the discrepancy in our expectations caused a disconnect that we had trouble identifying until we had a chance to talk it through after the race.

A friend of ours told a great story about the first few months of his marriage. His custom after dinner was to do chores—laundry, vacuuming, organizing, and general tidying up. But for his husband, the time after dinner had always been reserved for rest and relaxation. It took a building resentment toward his husband for them to finally have a conversation. His husband wasn't lazy, and our friend wasn't a neurotic clean freak; they simply had different expectations of how they were supposed to be spending their evenings.

We've become better at spotting instances in which we might have conflicting plans for something and then talking about them in advance. For example, if we're on our way to a party, one of us will typically ask, "What are your expectations for this evening?" If it's a gathering where we don't know a lot of people, we may agree to stay close to each other. If one of us is feeling tired, we may agree on a time that we'll leave. That way, no one is stuck stewing in a corner while the other is tearing up the dance floor past midnight.

Mismatched expectations are like pieces of uneven cement on a sidewalk—the further apart they are, the greater the danger they pose. But if we can spot them in advance, we can circumvent them before we trip up.

The Togetherness Tug-of-War

The first night apart is a rite of passage for most newly married couples. We experienced it about seven months into our marriage, when Constantino left town for a short business trip. He was sad to be away from home and told me how much he'd miss me. I (David), however, was relishing the idea of a night alone, already picking out my dinner (nachos from the greasy Mexican place down the street) and my evening's entertainment (the latest season of *The Great British Baking Show* on Netflix).

The trip highlighted our ongoing tug-of-war between intimacy and independence. Even though many of our wants overlap, there's a discrepancy in our needs for time together and time alone. This is a source of stress in our relationship that we still manage today.

Both of us are introverts, but we joke that Constantino is actually a "duovert," meaning he's an introvert who is able to recharge not only when he's by himself but also when he's alone with just his husband. To him, I am rest. Conversely, I'm more of a classic introvert: I like to be completely alone in order to recharge. As someone who has trouble connecting with my emotions, I need an absence of external stimuli to be able to identify my feelings and assess my internal well-being; otherwise, I become disconnected from myself.

Trouble arises either when I fall out of touch with myself or when Constantino is feeling empty or insecure in the relationship. The two problems are often related. If I ignore my need for independence for fear of hurting Constantino's feelings, the overabundance of intimacy begins to breed resentment. When I begin to feel crowded, I pull away emotionally in an attempt to give myself the space I need. The effect is that Constantino, who thrives on quality time and touch, senses that there's something wrong in the relationship. His way of repairing an emotional gap is to drive deeper into closeness, which is the opposite of what I need. And so the tug-of-war begins. It becomes a downward spiral that has resulted in harsh words and hurt feelings.

John Gottman invites couples to think of this struggle more like a tango than a tug of war. In *The Seven Principles for Making Marriage Work*, written by Gottman and Nan Silver, they explain that one partner often ignores the other not out of malice but because of their respective needs for intimacy and independence. "Marriage is something of a dance," they write. "There are times when you feel drawn to your loved one and times when you feel the need to pull back and replenish your sense of autonomy."[3] The potential for conflict arises when spouses fall on different points of the spectrum in terms of their needs. Some people desire more frequent connection, while others crave more independence.

Over the course of our marriage, we've been working at tugging less and dancing more. What has been most important is to lay positive groundwork; before we even address issues of independence and intimacy, we try to fill each other up daily with small affirmations and acts of affection. When we both feel emotionally full, it's easier to express our needs and accept the needs of the other. Then we try to identify and address our needs before we're in crisis mode.

We also work on building trust by making a request that includes a compromise. For example, I might say, "I want to go for a run alone this afternoon, but can we plan on watching a movie together tonight?" Or Constantino might say, "I'd really like for you to come with me to this dinner party on Saturday night, but you can do your own thing on Sunday." In that way, we're asking for what we want but also acknowledging the other person's need.

Now that we're more aware, we try to build in moments of intimacy and independence throughout our week before we're running at a deep deficit. We know this will always be a problem in our marriage, and we'll never do it perfectly. Because our needs are different, we know the tension between intimacy and independence will always exist. But we're trying to view it as a dance rather than a tug-of-war to remind us that this is a collaboration rather than a competition.

Space for Mistakes

When we first started dating, I (Constantino) had recently moved to Los Angeles and, like a good New Yorker, was determined to rely on public transit. I resisted for as long as I could, but finally I caved in to car culture. After a month of two-hour bus commutes to and from work, I desperately needed something to get me around town. David, who is always more practical, advised me to buy a reliable used Honda. But if I was going to get a car, I wanted something more exciting. I also didn't want to spend a lot of time shopping around. The first car I test-drove was a VW, and I decided to buy it on the spot. David had come along, and he strongly advised me against it, but I didn't listen. Sure enough, within a week, the car broke down, requiring the first of many expensive repairs.

What do we do when we can't stop our partners from making a decision we're certain is bad? Should we dig in our heels and oppose them until they change course? Or should we voice our concerns, then hold our peace and support them no matter the outcome? It's a matter of whether you want to be right, or whether you want to be successful in your relationship.

To be clear, we're not talking about enabling destructive behavior or relinquishing your stake on decisions that will severely impact your marriage and future together. But when it comes to the myriad minor decisions in life, we've found that sticking by your partner and supporting their choices is more important than preventing them from making mistakes.

Supporting each other even when you disagree is an important part of marital friendship, which is what keeps relationships strong over time—more so than great sex or deep romance. That friendship is strengthened when you extend grace to your spouse by refraining from speaking the dreaded "I told you so" when their ill-advised plans go exactly the way you warned they would.

Conversely, the marital friendship is weakened when a partner feels constantly criticized. It makes the relationship adversarial rather than collaborative. You might stave off a mistake, but it may be at the cost of damaging the friendship. In the long run, you'll lose.

Even when you disagree, rallying behind your spouse's decision and facing the consequences together makes you a stronger team. Taking your partner's side in solidarity, even when you think their perspective is wrong, communicates that you respect them and that you're willing to accept their influence. Most important, it reminds your spouse that you are taking on life together, no matter what the future may hold.

When my VW became a money pit, David refrained from reminding me of his advice to buy a reliable car. Instead, he patiently drove me to and from the repair shop. All these years later, I remember the car fiasco with gratitude for David rather than with bitterness over our disagreement. David was, first and foremost, a good and loving friend.

It's fair to note that I bought that car when we had only just started dating, so David was less attached to the outcome. Allowing each other's mistakes has gotten more difficult after marriage, perhaps because we are more intimately tied together and affected by each other's decisions. We always try to work toward consensus, but our diverging opinions are still abundant. Although this is very much a "choose your battles" situation, we like to think of it instead as "choose your peace." It's easier to let go of decisions when we know we are doing it to preserve peace.

Express your reservations with love, and if your spouse chooses not to listen, stand by them anyway. If need be, quietly help them out should they find themselves in a predicament. Proving that you're right doesn't make your marriage stronger, but being supportive does.

Repair, Repair, Repair

Marriage often feels as if it is subject to the rules of entropy, gradually declining into disorder if left to its own devices. When we don't actively maintain our relationship, Constantino tends toward insecurity and I (David) tend toward isolation. The result is an underlying disconnect that eventually erupts into an argument.

All couples fight. This is a fact supported by decades of research.[4] Our goal isn't to never argue, because that's an unrealistic expectation. And although we try to be respectful when we argue, our goal isn't to be so calm and polite that we'd fit in at high tea with the queen. It's healthy to express opinions and even more important to express emotions. What matters is not so much the argument itself, but what comes after. We've learned to become masters of repair attempts, employing them early and often to mollify each other before our disputes escalate.

A repair attempt is any statement or action—verbal, physical, or otherwise—meant to diffuse negativity and keep a conflict from escalating out of control. In *The Seven Principles for Making Marriage Work*, Gottman and Silver call repair attempts a secret weapon of emotionally intelligent couples. Their research shows that "the success or failure of a couple's repair attempts is one of the primary factors in whether [a] marriage is likely to flourish or flounder."[5]

Both of us are good at making repair attempts because we like to resolve conflict quickly. Early in our marriage, however, we realized that sometimes our repair attempts fell flat or, worse, they escalated the argument. We've come to realize that the success of a repair attempt often had to do with how well it was tailored to the other person.

For example, sometimes Constantino attempts to repair with physical touch by hugging or kissing me. This is one of his love languages,[6] and so he interprets touch as a way to express affection in the midst of conflict. I appreciate touch in general, but when I'm physiologically flooded my walls go up, and touch feels to me like an act of aggression. Even though I'm aware that Constantino's touch is a repair attempt, it feels like a violation.

One lesson Constantino has learned over time is that I respond well to humor, in part because I know I can be uptight about trivial things. So when I become snappish over something insignificant like dirty dishes, rather than trying to hug me, Constantino has taken to humoring me. He often does a little dance in which he points at me and in a funny voice starts calling me by my pet name (which we needn't mention here). The result invariably makes me laugh, and the conflict de-escalates even if the problem isn't immediately resolved. And when he's able and willing, Constantino also addresses my primary concern. He rolls up his sleeves and does the dishes.

What our marriage has taught us is that the simple act of making repair attempts isn't enough. Knowing how your partner receives love will help you devise ways to more effectively calm an argument. Maybe your spouse responds well to gifts, and so during a cool-down period after a fight you go buy him flowers or his favorite coffee drink from Starbucks. Maybe your spouse craves affirmation, and so during a fight you seek to reassure her of how much you love her, even when you're angry about something she did.

We've found that knowing your partner's love language is like having a secret weapon to mitigate conflict.

Of course, simply making a good repair attempt doesn't ensure success. It's also incumbent upon the other spouse to recognize and accept the attempt. And if only one person in a marriage is habitually making the effort to resolve conflict, the imbalance may take its toll over time. Both spouses need to do the work toward dissolving negativity and, when possible, resolving conflict.

For my part, I know that in the midst of conflict, Constantino will feel comforted with physical touch—a comforting hand on his knee or a gentle arm around him. Sometimes there might even be a shoulder rub involved. The magic is that once one partner makes a repair attempt, the other person feels better and usually responds in kind.

If you're like us, you'll have many petty disputes that seek to cast your marriage into entropy. We're developing effective tools to alleviate the conflict and get past it as quickly as possible so we can get back to staying connected. These efforts don't always come natural to us, but we've been learning that a significant part of love is simply making the effort to repair, maintain, and grow the relationship. Love might be work, but it helps to remember that the work *is* love.

Questions for Reflection

1. Do you and your partner have conflicts that stem from mismatched expectations? In what situations does this most frequently happen, and what steps can you take to avoid it?
2. Is one of you more independent than the other? How do you navigate your relationship so that the needs of both of you are met?
3. In what ways do you try to fix your partner? Do you feel as if your partner is trying to fix you? What is a better approach?

4. What are your conflict styles? How can you make your fights more constructive?
5. Have you experienced love to be work? Do you intentionally work on your relationship, or do you let it be? What are some advantages and disadvantages of each approach?

LESSONS IN MARRIAGE
FROM THE EXPERT

Dr. Julie Schwartz Gottman has been an advocate for same-sex relationships since long before marriage equality and before the Gottman Institute had become the world's leading organization for the research and study of marriage. She and her husband, John Gottman, have spent more than thirty years helping couples, both straight and gay, create and maintain greater love and health in their relationships.

As a self-identified feminist who is concerned with issues of social justice, Julie was willing to study homosexuality at a time when gay men and women were considered broken or deviant. While she was pursuing her PhD in clinical psychology in the early 1980s, she became aware of the way in which gay and lesbian parents were discriminated against in child custody cases. These parents typically lost custody during divorce proceedings because they were assumed to be unfit.

"It was a nightmare," Julie says. "The children would be taken away and given to alcoholic mothers or fathers, drug addicts, grandparents, uncles and aunts—anybody other than the gay or lesbian parent."

Judges at that time made rulings based on assumptions about what would happen if children were raised by a gay or lesbian parent—namely, that the child would grow up gay or gender-confused (which was considered bad)—even though there was no research to back up those assumptions.

"This was a travesty of justice," Julie says. "And being a nice Jewish girl, I'm very interested in justice in general and persecution in particular."

Julie performed the world's first controlled study on children being raised in the homes of lesbian moms. Her research looked at how daughters raised by their biological lesbian moms after a divorce turned out, as compared to daughters of divorce who were raised by heterosexual single moms or re-mated moms who found new male partners.

"What I found is there were no differences in sexual orientation between three groups of daughters, no differences in gender identity, and in social adjustment also no significant differences," Julie says.

The only trend she saw was that daughters raised in two-parent households, either gay or straight, had a stronger sense of well-being and security in the world compared to those raised by single parents.

In 2003, John Gottman released the findings of a years-long study of gay and lesbian couples he conducted with Robert Levenson. The study found that same-sex unions were comparable to heterosexual ones in satisfaction and quality but that there were slight differences in how gay couples interacted and handled conflict.

"What we saw is that [gay and lesbian] relationships tended to be a bit healthier than those of heterosexual couples," Julie says. "Gay men tended to be much more direct. In terms of conflict management, there was much less physiological flooding. There was more humor during their conflicts. They were often good friends, and they could talk much more directly about sex and therefore had more contented sexual relationships because they really understood each others' needs. For lesbians, much of that was the same."

What is it about same-sex relationships that makes them more resilient in the face of conflict? The study didn't offer conclusions about why, but the Gottmans have developed some possible ideas.

"The conjecture is that there's a lot of social conditioning that goes on for genders," Julie says. "Naturally [partners of the same gender] are going to understand each other a little bit better because they understand the social conditioning that each other has gone through. There is also less fear about being vulnerable. But we should take that with a grain of salt; it depends on the region and family culture in which each person was raised."

Julie says another reason same-sex couples are likely so resilient is because they have already had to face conflict with others as they have established their identity, and in the midst of rejection from family, church, and society, they create other support structures for themselves.

"Another part (of resilience) is that you have community," Julie says. "Because our culture is homophobic, most gay and lesbian couples have a group around them, if they're not too isolated, that pulls together because of social persecution. The culture out there can still be hostile and frightening. That outside negativity unites people, and there's research in groups such as church communities that shows that when a community is tightly knit, they help support marriages to stay together." This insight highlights the disservice done by "welcoming" but nonaffirming faith communities that allow same-sex couples to attend services but never accept them into the community.

Resilience is an important characteristic of a healthy relationship, even for the Gottmans themselves. As the authorities and experts on marriage, many couples expect them to have everything worked out in their relationship.

"People put us on a pedestal, that we should have the perfect marriage," Julie says. "So what we do, and we do this every time in our couples workshops, is to talk about how we are in the same soup as everybody else. In front of the audience, we process a regrettable incident that we've had, meaning a terrible fight that may end up with John sleeping on the couch. In this way we work hard to take ourselves off the pedestal and to say that everything we know we've learned from the couples who came through our lab. We try to put into practice what we've learned, but we're human too, and sometimes we fail and do a terrible job and have to repair it and work on it like everyone else."

The Gottman Institute has helped tens of thousands of couples improve and repair their relationships through workshops, books, and relationship checkups. Not everyone, however, has appreciated their evidence-based approach to relationship, in part because the method espouses an egalitarian approach to marriage. Julie recounts a time that an ultraconservative church in Texas began spreading nasty rumors about them to discredit them and their work.

"We were challenging the notion that men in opposite-sex relationships should have all of the power and all of the decision making and should never listen and be 'pussy-whipped' by their wives," she says. "We were also challenging that domestic violence is acceptable and saying that it's not OK for men to keep their women 'in line.'"

Although Julie has no statistics on how many same-sex couples have used the Gottman Method, she says that in a study conducted by two Gottman-Method couples therapists in San Francisco, Gottman-Method therapy proved highly effective in helping to strengthen the relationships of distressed gay and lesbian couples. Also, anecdotally, it appears that more gay and lesbian couples have sought out their resources as homosexuality becomes more widely accepted.

"We've noticed in the past three or four years, out of twenty-two years, we've had many more lesbian and gay couples coming to our workshops," Julie says. "Not as many gay guys; there may still be some fear about being in a primarily hetero audience. But I'm hoping more will come."

Julie's relationship advice:
"Honor each other's dreams. Ask each other questions about what gives your lives meaning and purpose. What are each partner's dreams within that life mission and purpose, and how can the other partner support them?"

CHAPTER 11

─────────── ∽◯∾ ───────────

INTERTWINED IN
INTIMACY

Weddings are strange things. As celebrated and exalted as they are across time and culture, they are relationally meaningless. That is to say, the relationship two people have the day before their wedding and the day after is the same; the wedding itself hasn't changed anything. Some would disagree, arguing that the spiritual covenant has transformed the two into one. It's a romantic notion, but two people don't simply meld together after a few words are spoken before an altar. If that were true, the divorce rate would not be as high as it is. The wedding vows are not a magical spell creating spiritual alchemy, but rather a promise of that alchemy. Two people may *technically* become "one flesh" by a covenant, but *practically* they become "one flesh" by the life that follows.

At the heart of this idea of "one flesh" is intimacy. It is something so primal, so deeply built into our DNA that our underlying need for connection drives every relationship in our lives. Each of us has a fundamental desire to know others and be known by them. A lack of intimacy is closely linked to depression, addiction, and illness.[1] But as much as we need it, many of us resist intimacy because of the vulnerability it requires. We may fear being known because we have experienced hurt or rejection in showing our true selves to others. Romantic relationship is an opportunity to let our guard down and relearn the reciprocal, mutually life-giving nature of healthy intimacy.

When people dream of marriage, it's often intimacy they are truly dreaming of. They probably have freeze-frame images in their mind of what life with a partner would look like: a lazy afternoon together in a coffee shop, cozy date nights in candlelit bistros, holiday traditions created together. But getting married doesn't create this intimacy—it's only an invitation into it. If we focus too much on the nuptials and those freeze-frame images, we won't be prepared for the hard work that true intimacy requires.

An example of this freeze-frame mindset came from one of David's friends, who fell deeply in love—with her wedding. It was a grand affair, to be sure: rustic chic in a converted barn, with bucolic views of green hills and twinkly white lights. Every detail had been thought through during the months of preparation. As with so many brides-to-be, the wedding became a veritable full-time job.

There were eight glorious hours of celebration, and then it was over. After her honeymoon, she seemed down. She was having trouble letting go of her activity on bridal websites, and she continued living vicariously through the weddings of other engaged friends she had made. There was a big, empty space in her life where a grand event had once stood. Their marriage began to falter not long after, in part because she may have been more attached to the dream of marriage than to the reality of married life. She resisted the work of intimacy.

We could have easily fallen into the same trap after our own wedding. After settling into our new life together, we felt "off" during the first month or two of marriage—a bit out of sync with the rest of life. We had caught a mild case of the postnuptial blues. Our funk had nothing to do with sadness about our wedding being past us. As magical a day as it was, we were both glad that it was over. It had to do with the direction and purpose the wedding provided. It gave us a mission; it was something for us to work toward.

After we returned from our honeymoon, when we were left with nothing but some wrinkled wedding programs and each other, we had no choice but to ask ourselves: *So now what?* There was one evening when we were lounging at home doing a lot of nothing. David quipped, "Well, just fifty more years of this." In one sense, fifty more years of cozy, serene evenings together sounded glorious. But we both knew what David was getting at: we could easily spend this same evening over and over, slipping into a lifetime of stagnation.

Up until that point, we had been focusing on a tangible benchmark for our relationship: marriage. With that past us, the future was wide open—too open. It lacked definition, like a long road disappearing into a fog. The fallacy of "happily ever after" does couples a disservice because it emphasizes a single point in a relationship rather than taking a long view.

We returned to some of the big questions we had asked ourselves before we got married, ones about our values and our expectations for life together. We talked again about our goals in terms of family, work, and dreams. And we talked about our relationship and how we wanted it to grow. After a few nights of discussion, that long, foggy road became a tiny bit clearer. We could see a few signposts instead of endless nothingness—aspirations we have for our lives and our family. Instead of walking aimlessly, we were walking toward something.

Marriage in Ordinary Time

One of the goals that came out of those discussions was to be intentional about growing deeper in relationship with each other. We had just exited a special season of life, and we wanted our daily lives to be just as meaningful. With the wedding behind us, we were entering a season of what we like to call Ordinary Time. In the liturgical calendar, Ordinary Time makes up the bulk of the year. It's everything other than the seasons of Christmas, Easter, Advent, and Lent.

Some would call Ordinary Time mundane, but these long stretches, when nothing especially noteworthy is happening, is when true intimacy occurs if we are intentional about it. Pearl Church's weekly bulletins remind us every Sunday of that season that, "Rather than meaning common or mundane, the term 'ordinary' (derived from the Latin root *ordo*) denotes ordered or counted time." *Ordered* and *counted* imply intentionality. These unremarkable seasons of life are when two people either grow together or grow apart. It's in the seemingly mundane that we have the opportunity to observe our loved one, like a character study, to deepen our understanding of them.

For example, a few months into our marriage, I (Constantino) was going through an especially stressful season of work and was having trouble getting out of bed one morning. David may not have noticed had we not been intentional the previous evening about sitting down at the dinner table and talking rather than eating in front of the television. Because of our conversation, David had background information about my state of mind, and he combined that with a few subtle clues (I got up for a long stretch in the middle of the night and then hit the snooze button multiple times in the morning). David could tell what was going on and, just as important, he knew how to comfort me. That morning he crawled into my bed and held me for a few minutes. That reminder that I had a secure base in my husband was all I needed to get myself up.

That gesture wasn't intuitive to David; it was learned over time. He isn't naturally touchy-feely, but he has lived with me long enough to understand my cues and to know how to respond to them. That kind of intimacy comes only from time spent together, from observing and letting yourself be observed.

Intimacy can be even more mundane than that. Knowing the way your partner takes their coffee, or their favorite place to eat, or their biggest pet peeves—all of these seemingly inconsequential bits of knowledge can become significant depending on how you choose to use them. Small actions in daily life can yield disproportionately large rewards: preparing a cup of coffee for your partner just how they like; bringing home takeout from a favorite restaurant after your partner has had a hard day; avoiding chewing with your mouth open or picking up your dirty laundry from the bathroom floor because you know those things drive your partner crazy. Data gathered during Ordinary Time has the potential to create deeper intimacy, but only if the partners are observant and willing to respond.

Knowing and loving each other in the day to day makes those extraordinary moments of life—both good and bad—all the more meaningful because they are shared with someone who is deeply invested in you.

One of the things I (David) love most about Constantino are the noises he makes. There's this little grunt he makes when he's angry or frustrated about something, like what I imagine comes from a burrowing hedgehog. Then there's the kind of mewing noise when he wants something he can't have, like when I make tzatziki for dinner and he wants to eat it right away. And then there are the sighs. He's a master of long, deep sighs, and like the Eskimo words for snow, there are a hundred different shades of meaning. To me, they're little sounds of music.

Part of what relationship affords is simply the choice to go deep with one person. It's a form of intimacy, ferreting out every little detail about another. Intimacy does not need to be romantic. If we believe we are all created in

God's image, we can discover beautiful divinity in anyone with whom we are willing to sit and gradually peel back the layers. But how much more meaningful is that process when it's with someone to whom we're uniquely committed? I'm glad Constantino and I met as adults and that we only dated for a year before becoming engaged. I learned enough about him to know that I wanted to spend my life with him, but there are still infinite, paper-thin layers for us to peel back in the coming years.

Contemporary culture is not accustomed to going deep. It's counter to our social-media existence, where abundance of relationship often supplants intimacy with a few. Most of us have become adept at casting a relationship net that is broad and shallow. Although quantity in itself is not a bad thing, we can never allow breadth to suffice for depth. Whether we are single or partnered, each of us must find that small circle of people willing to do a deep dive into relationship.

I like to think of Constantino as a complex piece of art, like one of those epic historical paintings that dominates an entire wall in a museum. There are moments when I take a broad view of him, when I see all of him and think I understand him. Then I'll get a glimpse of something in the corner, something I hadn't seen before, and I'll get really close. That little detail will surprise me, and I'll understand him—the entire painting—a little bit better. But I'm not merely an observer. A better analogy would be two paintings taking each other in. When I get close to see the details in Constantino, I can't help but reveal the details in myself as well. There's a mutuality to our observation.

What I love about going deep with Constantino is how reflective it is of my relationship with Jesus. It's easy and comfortable for me to take a broad view, to simplify my understanding of him to a children's Bible version. But Jesus isn't a finger painting. When I step close— uncomfortably close—he reveals details about his nature that I could never see from a distance. And when I'm that close to him, I can't help but reveal those vulnerable, intimate parts of myself as well. Jesus knows those details; he knows all my little sounds. My relationship with Constantino has taught me how to be more vulnerable in my relationship with God.

I wonder if there will ever be a day when Constantino and I communicate exclusively in grunts, mews, and sighs. I doubt we'll ever reach that level of telepathy, and I'm glad for it. That would mean that we had discovered every detail about each other, had figured out every thought. Essential to a thriving relationship is ongoing discovery, and I hope to find my husband time and again over a lifetime.

Making Space

There is, of course, such a thing as too much togetherness. As we wrote in chapter 10, everyone craves a different amount of intimacy, so two people will always dance back and forth on the spectrum of closeness and autonomy. If we spend too much time in the deep end of intimacy, one or both partners will soon feel like they're drowning.

Only six months after we got married, I (Constantino) accepted a job that had me working from home. David, a full-time fiction writer during that season, was already working from home in our tiny, one-bedroom apartment. If the thought of spending every waking and sleeping moment with your new spouse sounds romantic, let me disabuse you of that notion. Your spouse's endearing "little sounds of music" quickly become more agitating than fingernails on a chalkboard.

It's hard to have quality time when there's too much quantity, and we slowly started taking each other's presence for granted. For us, familiarity bred not so much contempt but discontent. A couple needs space to nurture their fondness and admiration for each other.

John Gottman and Nan Silver write that nurturing positive feelings for your spouse deepens intimacy and helps take the edge off conflicts when they arise: "Fondness and admiration can be fragile unless you remain aware of how crucial they are to the friendship that is at the core of any good marriage. By simply reminding yourself of your spouse's positive qualities—even as you grapple with each other's flaws—you can prevent a happy marriage from deteriorating."[2]

The key to nurturing fondness and admiration is getting in the habit of always looking for qualities you appreciate in your spouse. You can't afford to take each other for granted. It requires actively cherishing each other—thinking with pride about your spouse's gifts and talents, their inner and outer beauty.

"Cherishing," they explain, "is a habit of mind in which, when you are separated during the course of the day, you maximize thoughts of your partner's positive qualities and minimize thoughts of negative ones. This active focusing on your partner's merits allows you to nurture gratefulness for what you have instead of resenting what is missing. Many couples do not realize that they are neglecting to cherish each other."[3]

By this definition, cherishing requires separation and distance. It's impossible to reflect fondly upon your partner when you are ceaselessly interacting with them. You can't easily muse on someone while simultaneously interacting with the object of your musing.

Spending all day together was a threat to our intimacy even if we didn't see it at first. We weren't fighting, and we weren't growing contemptuous, but we were becoming complacent. Fortunately, we found a solution; a friend let me use some vacant office space so that I could leave the apartment during the day. Not only did we become more productive at our jobs, but we had the space to think of each other, to look forward to each other's company at the end of the day.

Getting (Financially) Naked

Intimacy is not merely about happy feelings and proximity. There are other, more practical kinds of closeness new couples have to navigate. For example, we chose not to live together before we got married, and moving in came with all of the hiccups intrinsic to sudden cohabitation: different organizational processes, different outlooks on chores, exposure to bodily functions and smells we hadn't had to experience of each other with such unfiltered reality. There was (and still is) occasional bickering over how to run the household, but we mostly settled into a routine that has worked for both of us.

What blindsided both of us early in marriage was not the difficulty in sharing space but in sharing finances. Growing up, I (David) was known as the family squirrel, storing up all of the quarters and dollars I earned from allowances and birthdays. When I was about six or seven years old, my sister and I received small metal cash boxes for Christmas, the cheap kind with a janky combination lock that's not really a combination because it opens on only one number.

After years of gifts from generous aunts and trips to take out the garbage, I had saved more than three hundred dollars in my little silver cash box—a small fortune for a kid. This was *my* money. I relished the freedom to do what I wanted with my money, even if it meant hoarding it. Money became a vehicle for autonomy.

Flash forward thirty years, and I still had a kind of cash box, only it had a different name—Bank of America—and it was substantially larger and more secure. Money allowed me to live on my own for years. It afforded me the ability to take trips when and where I wanted. Independence was my goal, and money was the means.

So when Constantino and I got married, sharing finances felt like a direct attack on my independence. I struggled with the concept of *my* money becoming *our* money. It wasn't the sharing of money that was the hardest part, but the sharing of decisions about how that money was spent or saved. For example, I once wanted to make plans to buy a plane ticket to visit an old friend. When I approached Constantino about it, I had already worked out the dates, found the flight, and figured out how it would work within our budget. And although I technically asked my husband before buying the ticket, I really only *informed* him about the trip. Rightfully, he felt cut out of the decision-making process.

Constantino struggled with money and marriage in a different way. Having been in a long-term relationship, he wasn't bothered by blending finances. His partner had managed their joint bank account, and Constantino never really thought about money unless they were short on it. Living in New York as young adults, it seemed as if everyone was subsisting paycheck to paycheck. It was the *la bohème* lifestyle.

Furthermore, Constantino grew up in a household that was historically wealthy but not wise about money. Because money was not traditionally in short supply, Constantino was never taught the importance and value of managing it. Even after some investments left his parents hurting financially, the family in some ways still operated as if they had their previous wealth.

Once we started dating, I pressured Constantino into a strict budget against his will. For him, it was like being forced to wear new shoes that didn't fit. He wasn't an extravagant spender, but he had little interest in tracking where every dollar went. It was tedious. He didn't see budgeting as a way toward financial freedom; he saw it as a burden that made him feel like a slave to his wallet. We had many arguments after Constantino would promise to track his spending but then would shut down emotionally and abandon the budget altogether.

Getting married and blending finances only upped the intensity of these conversations. Each of us felt as if he were losing his freedom in some way. It's no wonder money arguments are a top predictor of divorce.[4] We were sure that blending bank accounts was the right choice for us, but it forced months of difficult conversations. Other couples prefer to keep their finances separate, and there are good cases to be made for each arrangement. Joint accounts foster trust, cooperation, and transparency—all of which are important components of a healthy marriage. Separate accounts, on the other hand, provide autonomy and minimize feelings of control or subordination.

We settled on a mixed approach. Our paychecks both go into a joint account, which we use to pay bills, buy groceries, eat out, and plan vacations. It makes keeping track of the family budget easier and allows us to quickly diagnose our family's financial health. At the same time, we keep separate individual accounts, which we each manage on our own. We both receive a monthly allowance that gets transferred to our individual accounts, and how we spend that money is none of the other's business. Which arrangement works best for you will depend both on practical as well as philosophical matters, and you shouldn't be afraid to revisit your arrangement down the line if you find that it is causing your marriage to struggle rather than flourish.

Regardless of what approach you choose, baring your finances for the first time is about as comfortable as standing naked on stage, even if it's with the person you love most. Constantino was forced to face the shame of student loan debt he had trouble getting under control. David was forced to concede ways in which his financial stability was not so much a result of his own merits but rather the way in which his parents set him up for success. This is intimacy at its most uncomfortable.

Talking about money is intimate because it means talking about who you are and what you desire. You have to ask yourselves: What do we want for our lives right now? What do we want for our lives in the future? What do we value most, and how can we make our spending reflect that? These big-picture conversations help you understand each other better and shed light on your reasons for spending the way you do. They also help to drive your daily decisions about finances.

Conversations about money continually force us to talk about dreams. What starts off as an unassuming talk about dollars and cents soon turns into deep heart-to-hearts about having children, going on vacations, supporting our church, experiencing job promotions and losses, growing old together, getting sick, and, ultimately, dying.

At our wedding, we gave ourselves to each other "until death do us part," but in the moment it's difficult to understand what that really means. Only life lived together after a wedding can reveal to you what it's like to continually turn toward each other in every aspect of your relationship, from the mundane to the extraordinary. Often this turning toward is a joy; at other times it will be the hardest thing you have ever done.

Intimacy is not a place at which you arrive and then settle in together for the rest of life. Rather, it is a path you choose to walk together, sometimes hand in hand, sometimes scowling at each other on opposite sides of the road. It's in the experience of the journey together—as the long road through life changes in scenery and climate and elevation—that true spiritual alchemy takes place.

Questions for Reflection

1. If you're a couple headed toward marriage, what do you envision life to be like after your wedding? What joys do you imagine, and what struggles do you anticipate?
2. Most people imagine what the picture-ready, "Instagram" moments of their relationship will be like. What do you imagine the day-to-day, mundane aspects of living together to be like?

3. How do you define intimacy? Is there such a thing as too much intimacy? What level of intimacy are you comfortable with?
4. Do you see finances as being intimate? As a couple, how have you (or how will you) navigate finances together?
5. How do you see intimacy with your partner changing over time?

CHAPTER 12

⚭

A LONG BUSINESS

In talking to one of her younger relatives, Violet Craw-
ley, the fictional matriarch of the British television show
Downton Abbey, says, "Marriage is a long business. There's
no getting out of it for our kind of people."[1] Well, we're
not *their* kind of people. But we *are* the kind of people
for whom marriage is a long business; there's no getting
out of it for us either. To us, marriage is more than just a
government-recognized contract. We don't see it as merely
a mutual agreement from which the two parties involved
can at any point release each other. We believe the bond of
kinship created by marriage comes not from the state but
from God. And God creates this bond not by serving only
as a witness, or by offering a simple blessing from above,
but as an actual party to the covenant.

In our view, a Christian marriage covenant involves
three beings rather than two. In addition to the promises
made by the couple to each other, there are independent
promises made by each spouse to God, and a promise made
by God as well. This is what emboldened Paul's assertion
in 1 Corinthians 7:4 that, in marriage, it is not we who

have authority over our own bodies, but our spouse. That claim—particularly the egalitarian teaching that "likewise the husband does not have authority over his own body, but the wife does"—must have shocked Paul's audience. Coming from one of the strongest advocates for singleness, and in a patriarchal culture where polygamy was the norm, telling a man that his wife (singular) had authority over his body signaled the importance of taking their marriage covenant seriously. It signaled that marriage is about more than just the desires of the individuals themselves.

We chose a traditional liturgy for our wedding because it unambiguously establishes the marriage covenant to be among three parties. The day we got married, before making any promises to each other, we stood individually before God and our church and stated that we "freely and unreservedly" offered ourselves to the other. We promised God that we would live "in the covenant of marriage, in faithfulness and holiness of life as long as we both shall live."

Then our church—the body of Christ—stood in the spirit of Matthew 18:18 and answered on God's behalf, establishing God's, and their, covenant with us: they vowed to uphold and honor our marriage, respecting the covenant we made, praying for us in times of trouble, and celebrating with us in times of joy.

It was only after we had each exchanged those vows with God that we made our promises to each other. We vowed to support, care, hold, cherish, honor, and love one another by the grace of God, in the love of Christ, and with the Spirit's help. Invoking the Trinity with our vows was an admission that we will always need the Divine's help in keeping them, and, most important, a reminder that our commitment is not only to each other, but to God.

The difference between the covenant we entered and the mere signing of a contract at a court is that we can't just give each other an out. We came together in mutual agreement, and that continues to this day. The day we got married we were in love. We joined hands at the altar because we make each other happy; we serve each other well. But there have also been days since our wedding when we haven't felt much love, when we've made each other angry, when being married feels like nothing but work. We haven't gotten to the point where either of us would consider separation, but there might be a day when we both do. Legally, we'd be allowed to divorce. If our vows were only to each other, no one would be able to stop us. But the individual promises we have made to God compel us to work through our problems long after we feel like quitting.

There's a misconception that same-sex couples fought for marriage because they just want to be affirmed and validated, but what most LGBTQ Christians long for is not simply affirmation, but rather an opportunity to grow, serve, and be living parts of the body of Christ. What we and others like us need is a place where we can be challenged, nurtured, and pushed toward growth, toward more awareness of the other, toward greater empathy for our proverbial neighbor. If you're married, that starts with your spouse.

As we discuss in chapter 14, a good marriage is outwardly focused; it carries a mission and seeks to make the world a more loving, peaceful place. That requires commitment and working together even when things get rough. That three-party covenant we described forms a triangle pointing the two partners to God. Pointing them, that is, to something greater than themselves: to the gospel truth of Christ incarnate, of God within us, within our neighbor, within the downtrodden and marginalized, and even within those with whom we disagree.

This is a lofty vision of marriage, one that requires those who enter into it to examine their reasons carefully. Yet it is also a more humble view of it than the one held by a majority of Christians, and perhaps even society at large, today. Marriage is not a grand institution, but merely a tool God has given us to work for the advancement of the kingdom founded by Jesus; a kingdom that is, in the words of Pearl Church's mission statement, "the consummation of peace in a world integrated by love." And as we said in chapter 5, it is not a tool needed by everyone, for some are equipped to do that work in singleness as they cultivate meaningful community outside of romantic relationship.

There's a stereotype about a certain type of straight woman who dreams of a big wedding and fixates on that day as the pinnacle of life. Within a month of her engagement, her Instagram profile consists of nothing but dozens of pictures of herself displaying her two most valued trophies: the ring and the man who bought it. She takes a condescending tone every time she talks to one of her single friends, and says things like "I'm sure you'll find someone too." Everyone finds her annoying, yet most people seem to buy into the premise behind her view of marriage as some kind of achievement. The male and LGBTQ versions of her exist as well, even if they are not caricatured as often. You could even say that she has been embodied by the church itself.

Our culture has set up marriage as one of life's ultimate benchmarks. Turn on the TV and soon you'll see it: the commercial in which a man and woman fall in love, buy a home, and fill it with children—all in thirty seconds. It's the trifecta of adulthood. We've coined it the three P's of maturity: partnership, property, and progeny. We might throw in some custom benchmarks (international travel, degrees in higher education, a specific job title), but the three P's comprise the standard checklist by which our culture gauges whether or not we've "arrived" as adults. But here's a secret: no matter how hard you try to check everything off that list, you'll never arrive.

Although neither of us really expected to marry, we both still looked at our married friends with a degree of longing. It wasn't just for the partnership, but the self-worth we imagined came with the marriage covenant.

We saw marriage as evidence that proved someone had reached a certain level of emotional maturity. As long as we remained single, we feared being caught in a kind of arrested development—boys trapped in men's bodies.

We're now married and have bought a house. We've attained two of the P's. We can finally say, even as we approach middle age, that we are adults. Yet instead of proving our emotional preparedness, the daily experience of marriage has shown us all of the ways in which we are inadequate: Not good enough listeners? Check. Oblivious to each others' true needs? Check. Always trying to fix each other? So many checks.

Rather than substantiating our adulthood, marriage has illuminated many of the ways in which we fall short. In reality, then, these benchmarks don't prove any level of maturity. They're more like stress tests that point out our weaknesses. If you're the kind of person who thrives on self-improvement, that's a good thing. The responsibilities of marriage, children, and homeownership will give you an unfiltered, unembellished look into your soul. And it's often not pretty.

Conversely, there's no reason to believe that those who haven't unlocked these achievements are any less far along in their maturity. This is where the church repeatedly gets it wrong; it honors the traditional family unit as the Christian ideal, the thing to which we must all aspire. Consequently, this becomes reflected in church leadership, where we see the family man as the only valid "shepherd" of the community with women, youth, and single people as the "flock" in need of shepherding. But marriage and children require no certifications or training. Indeed, some of the wisest, most mature people we know lack all three P's.

These milestones our culture has established are merely life circumstances that have only tangential associations to our maturity. We believe God cares about our circumstances, but the Divine's true investment is in how we develop in response to and regardless of the circumstances.

God is cultivating the hearts of all who will allow it, but we don't all develop in the same way. Some plants grow, flower, and die all in one year. Others take years before they blossom. Still other plants, like ferns, never flower but are some of the oldest and most resilient organisms on earth. There is no metric for comparing which is better.

Whether you're single or recently engaged, don't make the mistake of seeing marriage as a prize to attain. Marriage is not the summit upon which you'll live happily ever after. Marriage is a lifelong commitment to grow and work with one another toward what the Jewish tradition calls *tikkun olam:* the healing of the world or, the interpretation we like best, a "construction for eternity." Each of us—married, single, cis, trans, gay, straight, black, white, rich, poor—has a unique and vital role in the construction of eternity, and not one role is more important than another.

If you are married, discern with your spouse the ways in which God is calling you to work together for what in Christianity we call the advancement of the kingdom. You'll be working on it for a very long time.

Questions for Reflection

1. Have you viewed marriage as a kind of achievement or accomplishment? If so, what are the ways in which that outlook can be damaging to you or others?
2. What other benchmarks in life do you feel compelled to "achieve"? How can you let go of that framework for seeing your life?
3. We believe a Christian marriage covenant involves three beings: the two spouses and God. Have you ever thought of the covenant in this way? What's your response?
4. Does inviting God into the marriage covenant change your approach and attitude toward marriage?

CHAPTER 13

───────── ⤫⤬ ─────────

CONTEMPLATING PARENTHOOD

Avoiding an approach to life that treats it as a checklist is easier said than done. After getting married and buying a house, we caught ourselves eyeing the checkboxes again and thinking of the next one: parenthood. The problem is that those who live by the checklist die by it too. There is always another item that needs a tick mark: a promotion, a vacation home, grandchildren. This view of life feels like riding up an infinite escalator, waiting to get to a platform that will never arrive. We've realized that the only way the escalator will ever end is to step off.

The topic of children is especially problematic in conservative and religious circles because many believe the purpose of marriage *is to have children*. There is no decision to be made, except perhaps when and how many. We have straight Christian friends who have thoughtfully chosen not to have children, and the response from others has ranged from confusion to sadness to subtle derision. Couples who choose not to have children are sometimes accused of being selfish, which is, of course, absurd. There's nothing selfless about creating a being that is wholly dependent on you because that need *does not exist* until you create it. No one creates a child for the betterment of society, but rather to fulfill their own dreams about life and family. We'd argue that both roads have an equal capacity for selfishness and selflessness. Both paths have the potential to be God-honoring.

LGBTQ marriages shatter the notion that marriage functions primarily as a social container to hold children, and that is one reason they have been received with such vitriol in conservative and evangelical communities. As we reflected on our vows and on the view of marriage that first brought us together, we realized that we are not sure at this point if parenthood is in the books for us. Having gotten married in our late thirties, we've been feeling pressured to make a decision. Men don't have the same kind of biological clock that women do, but our joints still creak and pop a little more with each passing year. We've had to remind ourselves: marriage is indeed a long business. It is meant to last well beyond the years we might spend raising children. Our commitment and our covenant are primarily to and with each other. We didn't marry in order to raise children. We married because we wanted to bind ourselves to each other and, together, discern and heed any callings God might have for us.

The pressure we'd been feeling also eased when we remembered that we share a perhaps unconventional view of parenthood. We don't see it as an achievement any more than we do marriage. And we don't think parents can take much credit or assume responsibility for the paths their children take as adults. We believe who we grow up to be may have more to do with our nature and inherent personality than with our parents' efforts to mold us. This isn't to say we don't think environment matters, but it does mean we would understand our limitations as parents and try to release ourselves from the pressure of believing that every decision we would make about our children would have lifelong consequences. The best philosophy we've heard about parenting came from a friend who is raising five kids. Rather than trying to shape them, she said, "I only want to get to know them. My goal is to discover who they are." The admission that her children, like all human beings, are a mystery—that they are not clay she will form but are already formed persons who will bear God's image in their own unique way—resonated with us. That's all we'd ever hope to get from parenting too: an intimate window into lives that will teach us things about God we couldn't learn on our own.

Any children we invite into our lives will be passengers on *our* drive, hitching a ride along with us on the way to their own journeys. You don't hand the wheel over to hitchhikers; you simply help them get safely to where they are going and hopefully enjoy the time spent together. If we decide to have children, it will alter the nature of our shared ride, but it won't determine the road or the destination. Realizing this has been freeing, particularly for Constantino, whose feelings about this issue have been the most fraught.

Grieving the Path Not Chosen

I (Constantino) always wanted to be a father. Before I met David, I was seriously considering single parenthood and had even started researching what it would take to go through surrogacy. At the time, I was much less stable and settled than I am now. Raising a child back then, in New York on a humble income, would have been much harder than it would be now. Yet the prospect seemed more appealing. This change of heart has caught me by surprise.

I remember sitting down at a coffee shop once when I was thirty-one or thirty-two and writing a letter to my future son. It was a particularly hard time in my life, and I wanted to capture what I was going through so I could share it with him when he grew up. I envisioned myself handing him the letter on his thirtieth birthday. The thought of sharing that with him, at an age when he might relate, gave me great comfort. And, I dreamed, it might someday give him comfort too—if he found himself facing similar questions. I dreamed of the conversations we would have, wherein I'd communicate to him that whatever troubles he was facing were just temporary, that they would pass, and that he would find happiness and stability—that he would find himself.

That wasn't the first letter I wrote to that theoretical future son. I remember also writing him one in my mid-twenties. I lost both of those notes during a move a few years later. But I don't mourn their loss, because what I recognize now is that they weren't so much letters I wanted my son to read but letters I yearned to read myself. The fact that both were addressed specifically to a son is telling. They were letters I wished my father had written me. It is evident now that my desire to be a father was intricately woven with my desire to be a son. I wanted to have a son I could know and see, because I wanted to be known and seen myself.

Growing up I was very close to my grandfather, Papa-ché. He and my grandma lived next door to us, so I saw him every day. My dad (his son) was a good and loving father, but Papaché was retired, so he simply had more time available for me. He always treated me with respect and encouraged me to develop intellectually. It didn't feel like he had an agenda, and it never felt as if he were trying to make me be—or not be—anything. I was only twenty when he died, and although he was ninety-two, I'll always feel like we were cheated out of time. I miss him still, but I missed him the most when I was younger and desperately needed the comfort and counsel of a father—the comfort and counsel that my coming out had made impossible to receive from my dad.

I have now mourned the loss of both my fathers: Papaché to death, and my dad to unsurpassable emotional barriers.

I treat my scars tenderly, but with time and the salve I've found in David, the wounds have closed. I feel truly that God—through love and covenant—has healed me. And I think this is why I no longer yearn for fatherhood the way I did when I was younger.

I would be lying if I said the thought of not having children doesn't sadden me. It does. I even think I would be better at parenting now than I would have been ten years ago. And I grieve deeply to think that I may never get to see David as a father, because I know he would be so good. I have full confidence in our ability to parent well; I think in that, as in most other things, we would make a great team. But it is also true that I'm not sure parenthood would improve our lives at this point. I know that whichever future we choose, we will grieve the loss of the path not chosen. In my mind I have images of what life would look like both with and without children. In one future I see exotic travel, meaningful service to church and community, space for creative projects, and deep investment in people I might not otherwise have time for; in the other future I see playful roughhousing, family dinners, teachable moments, and feelings of indescribable pride as our children become self-sufficient adults. Both futures are appealing, but we can't live two lives.

I don't think I want to have a child in the next year or two, but I also fear the ways having a baby in our mid-forties (who would be a teenager when we're in our sixties!) would disrupt our lives. I fear that the opportunity cost of parenting at our age is no longer worth it. And so I wonder if, despite the undeniable sadness that would come with a decision to not have children, David and I are not better off just mourning that loss together, holding each other in our grief, and looking forward to what other missions God may have for us.

Most couples feel the pressure to check things off a list—to get married, buy a house, have kids, and start dressing them up for photo shoots. But there's a subtle way in which the stakes can feel higher for LGBTQ Christian couples. The sanctity of our unions has already been challenged so fiercely that many of us may feel as if we must have as close to a traditional, picture-perfect family as possible. More so than secular couples, we may be afraid of "queering" marriage too much because any further deviation from the norm can lead others to question our standing before God. Yet the decision to have children is one where we, unlike most straight couples, have no choice but to be intentional—no same-sex couple will ever have a child together by accident. Let us welcome that forced intentionality and discern carefully what is truly best for each of our marriages.

Questions for Reflection

1. Have you given much thought to parenthood? What are your reasons for wanting to be a parent?
2. Do you feel pressure to have children or to have what looks like a traditional family unit? Where does that pressure come from?
3. Have you talked about children with your partner? What if one of you wants children and the other doesn't? What if both of you think you want children but one of you changes their mind after marriage?
4. What do you picture your parenting style to be like, and how will it complement or contrast the style of your partner?

An Interview with Paula Williams

CRCRD

TRANSITIONING AFTER FORTY YEARS OF MARRIAGE

By all accounts, Paula Williams had been living a life that checked off every box on the list of success: she had three beautiful children, a wife she adored, and a high-profile job leading one of the world's largest church-planting organizations. But back then she was living as Paul, a man. And her gender dysphoria—the term used for the distress a person feels when the gender they were assigned at birth doesn't match their gender identity—caused her to be severely depressed. After forty years of marriage, and with the support of her family, Paula transitioned.

Paula had been a twenty-one-year-old student at a Bible college when she married her wife, who was nineteen. "In fair measure," she says, "we got married at that age because that's what you do in the world we grew up in, and because you can't have sex until you get married, and so you get married." She adds that they weren't ready. They were much too young.

Looking back, Paula appreciates how good she and her ex-wife were at parenting. They have three grown kids, and she's proud of how well they've all done. In terms of their relationship, however, there are things that she would like to have done differently. "I wish someone had told us that love was not falling in love," she says. "Love is something different. It was, I think, probably fifteen years into my marriage that I realized that falling in love is just a temporary lowering of ego boundaries. It's built into our species through evolution to make sure we get married, because if we truly kept our ego boundaries up and saw the other clearly, nobody in their right mind would ever get married. It's the whole falling in love that allows us to deny reality for a period of time before we have to come to realize that the other person is screwed up, and that we're screwed up."

In Paula's telling, people spend the first ten years of marriage trying to straighten out their spouse and trying to fix what's wrong with *them*. Then they spend the next fifteen finding out that the problem isn't really their spouse, but themselves. "So it's twenty-five years into the marriage that, now, you can actually begin working on the relationship," she observes. "Because it was neither your spouse, nor was it you."

Eventually, Paula and her ex-wife began to see marriage under a different light from the one shone on it by their families and peers. Rather than seeing themselves as two halves of one whole, they understood themselves to be two wholes, coming together to form a third entity. "We had four entities in our family outside of ourselves," she explains. "We had three children, and we had the relationship. And of all of those four, the one that was going be around longer was the relationship. The three children would someday be eighteen and go off on their own; the relationship would continue, we thought, until death."

They saw that fourth entity—their relationship—as their "base camp." From it, each of them would go off and climb their own mountains. One of Paula's mountains was her gender dysphoria, which she shared with her wife early on. However, Paula grew up in an era when she didn't think transitioning could ever be an option. Her hope had been that marriage would "fix" her. "Very little was known at that point," she says, "so we just thought this was something we were going to have to navigate."

They didn't see it as too much of a threat to their marriage because, as Paula explains, unlike trans men—who usually identify as bi or as lesbians prior to transition—most trans women are attracted to women. In other words, Paula knew she wasn't a gay man, so being married to a woman didn't feel unnatural.

It wasn't until some thirty years into their marriage that Paula began to realize that she was in fact transgender. "That's when I began to realize that maybe I would have to transition. I didn't want to. I didn't want to do that to my family. I was very committed to not doing it—not because I thought it was wrong or sinful, but because I didn't want to do that to our relationship."

The decision to transition and to dissolve their marriage at their age was, understatedly, difficult for Paula and her ex-wife. But she says they are closer now than they were during their last decade of marriage. The fact that they have remained close is a testament to the friendship they had built and the mindful way in which they nurtured their relationship during the decades they spent together. "What you usually see," says Paula, "is either a wife leaving furious because she had never known—and truly, most of the time they have no idea—or a wife who stays because she has never differentiated as a human. What you see more rarely is a couple that remains close, but they do split up."

Paula shared with us a bittersweet memory of their last session with their marriage therapist. He was retiring, and they were the last couple he saw on his last day. "I asked him, 'How many couples are willing to work this hard?' And he said, without hesitation, 'One percent.'

And I said, 'How many couples get this far?' And he said, 'One percent—which is what makes this so tragic, because you're a lesbian and she's not.' And that was the difficult reality of our setting. All our therapists kept saying this was tragic, because we were good people and were trying so hard to make things work. But 'tragic' wasn't helpful. We needed to find a way to move forward, and in our case it meant moving forward in separate ways." So they did.

Paula says she would like to find the kind of partnership she had with her ex-wife, and she doesn't rule out dating and finding someone new. But at an age when most of her peers are looking at retirement, transitioning has imbued her with newfound energy. And God, it seems, has called her to a new mission. Having spent decades at the helm of one of the nation's largest evangelical church-planting organizations, Paula has now dedicated her life to making the church a safe and nurturing environment for LGBTQ people. She serves as pastor of preaching and worship ministries at Left Hand Church, an open and affirming congregation in Colorado; she is codirector of Launch, a church-planting ministry; and she serves on the board of directors for the WITH Network and Q Christian Fellowship.

Paula's relationship advice:
"Treat your marriage as an additional child. If you don't have children, treat your marriage as your one child. Treat it as an entity that needs its own special attention throughout life, because otherwise you will drift apart."

CHAPTER 14

―――――――――― ⦚⦚ ――――――――――

RELATIONSHIP
AS MISSION

There's a plot device in fiction and film called a "MacGuffin," which is employed most often in thrillers, action movies, and adventure stories. A MacGuffin is a valuable object or an important goal that motivates the protagonists but is ultimately inconsequential to the story itself. The Holy Grail is perhaps the most infamous MacGuffin in Western culture, providing a motivating call to action for the heroes of Arthurian literature. Whether or not the Grail is actually found does not matter so much as the trials that take place on the grand quest and the subsequent development of the heroes who endure them. The story is the journey itself, not what lies at the end.

Whether consciously or not, successful marriages employ their own MacGuffins to give their relationship both motivation and meaning. This can take the form of hobbies, traditions, symbols, or goals. There's the couple obsessed with a particular sport, who play it together, watch their team on TV, and like to praise and criticize the professional athletes. Many of us are familiar with the husband and wife devoted to their church, who are there more days of the week than not, volunteering in every ministry. And many couples, of course, find shared meaning in having children, helping them develop into self-sustaining human beings.

Marriages thrive on purpose and direction. But how much better is it when that purpose has substance? How much more motivating is a MacGuffin that seeks to leave the world a better place? Any kind of shared meaning is better than none, but the best kind is an outwardly focused, altruistic, shared mission. It shifts the perception that marriage is something insular and inwardly focused to something that gives life to the wider community. Antoine de Saint-Exupéry, author of *The Little Prince*, put it best: "Love does not consist in gazing at each other, but in looking outward together in the same direction."[1]

Part of the reason we fell in love with each other was because we saw in the other person a desire for shared mission. When Constantino was courting me (David), at a time when I was still uncertain I was prepared to be in a same-sex relationship, he made a most convincing argument: "Think of how our relationship could touch friends and family around us," he said. "Imagine the good we could do simply by living our lives openly and sharing our story." That may not sound romantic to many people, but it touched my heart more than roses or chocolates ever would. Doing life together with a shared mission sounded more exciting and alluring than mere companionship. It was love, fortified by another, and then turned outward. We had no idea at the time what that might look like; we only knew that we wanted our relationship to have a purpose beyond serving and pleasing each other.

At the time, Constantino was considering becoming an Episcopal priest, and we imagined a life serving a church community together in this way. I was getting used to the idea of becoming a pastor's husband when life took us in a different direction. We began to document our journey of engagement and marriage because, as writers, we can't help but write. As people began to respond to our story by reflecting on their own—both the struggles and the joys of LGBTQ relationship at all of its stages—we began to see that our mission was something already built into us. Our relationship itself was the mission, and the tools were our words.

What is your purpose as a couple? What is your mission? For some, it may be a natural extension of the work you do. We're friends with a gay couple who built a fire lookout tower in the middle of the Oregon forest (yes, the same one in which we got engaged). They turned their short-term vacation rental business into a mission of hospitality. They host parties throughout the year for former guests and have built a unique community of travelers. Other friends of ours, a straight married couple, work together in the filmmaking industry as a director-producer duo, and they inspire the world by telling meaningful stories that shape how we see others and ourselves.

You might also find mission through your shared passions. While doing a walk across the United States, Constantino wrote about a couple he met in Richmond, Virginia, who have a heart for people who are displaced.[2] Not only do the two men have six adopted children, but they turned their home into a ten-bedroom sanctuary for friends down on their luck and even local day laborers with nowhere to stay. Another couple we know has a passion for both fitness and refugees; they started a gym in Portland that is intentionally inclusive of the local immigrant and refugee community, including a women-only class that is sensitive to the cultural dress standards set for Muslim women. Still another couple we know developed a passion for helping others succeed in marriage after they saw many of their friends get divorced; they began to discuss the challenges and joys of marriage from a heterosexual perspective on a blog and podcast called #*staymarried*.

Many of us have difficulty finding our own individual calling, much less a mission together as a couple. It may take time growing together before you can see what is unique about your relationship and how it functions in the world. We're always on the lookout for themes: topics we frequently find ourselves talking about, issues that make both of us angry or sad, gifts or wounds that we both share. Therein lies the potential for shared mission.

A couple may share multiple missions, and the missions may change over a lifetime. For example, we believe all Christian LGBTQ couples have, at this particular moment in time, a unique built-in purpose of reconciliation if they choose to assume the mantle. In faith-based circles especially, LGBTQ marriages have the power to transform hearts and minds in a way nothing else can. Many Christians still see us as the "other," an aberration to be, at best, ignored or, at worst, exterminated. Christian LGBTQ marriages witness to the radical nature of God's love by the mere nature of their existence. Not every couple will be called to activism, but each of us has a story worth telling, if only we are willing. If you're in a faith-based queer relationship, this call to action isn't a mandate; it's an invitation. But the world will be so much richer if you accept the call to adventure and boldly share your story with those around you.

For many of us who rejected our attractions or gender identities for years, it's a long transition to not only accepting these parts of ourselves but embracing them as something we acknowledge as vital threads in the tapestry of the human story. Many of us have wounds that cut deep, but we've come to realize that the experience of bleeding helps us better empathize with a God incarnate who bled and died for us. Wounds hurt, and they can destroy, but it's also through wounds that we can see what's inside each other. Within our deepest hurt lies our deepest strength. That might be why Jesus rose from the dead not with a body that was perfectly healed, but one with wounds that Thomas was able to see and touch.

For this reason, we're so grateful that we are part of the LGBTQ community. Being gay has given us the opportunity to grow into kinder people who are better attuned to the plights of others. Even with those whose experiences and hurts are far different from ours, who have been marginalized or ostracized in other ways, our hearts are better attuned to their suffering. That is not to say we are perfectly actualized people. Our hearts are still learning, ever peeling back the layers to understand and empathize better with others who are unlike us.

After decades of wishing and praying the gay away, we've finally reached a point in life where we honor it as something essential to our development as human beings. When we try to imagine our lives otherwise, we can't connect with the selves who might have been. Both of us were raised in well-respected, loving, financially stable homes. We're both cisgender men and, although Constantino is an immigrant from Guatemala and David is the son of an Arab immigrant, we're both white. We both grew up with a wealth of privileges we took at face value. Growing up this way is a gift, but it comes with blind spots. It did wonders for our self-development, but there was little motivation for us to look outward beyond our immediate class and culture. The closer you are to the center of what is mainstream, the harder it is to see people on the fringes. If there hadn't been a part of us that society cast out, we may never have gone on the journey to the fringes to retrieve it. And that journey to the outskirts to reclaim a part of ourselves was as valuable as any quest to find the Holy Grail.

Erasing Otherness

No matter where we exist in society, each of us is susceptible to diminishing the other. I (David) was reminded of this one day while I was walking home from the gym and passed a dead bird on the sidewalk. It was a baby bird, not quite a fledgling, that looked as if it had fallen out of its nest. One leg was crooked, and there were a couple of flies on it. I cringed, stepped past the carcass, and muttered one word to myself: *gross*.

I walked half a block, stopped, and turned around. I'm not sure why. Maybe I figured I would kick it away from the sidewalk or find a piece of cardboard to scoop it into a nearby trash can. When I returned, the bird was still there, motionless, accumulating more flies. I bent over and, on a hunch, blew softly on it. The bird moved. It fluttered its fuzzy wings and kicked its little legs, even the one that looked broken. It shook the flies off itself and opened its beak, gasping for air.

In that moment, my whole perception of the bird shifted. It was not something disgusting to be kicked aside or thrown in the trash. It was a creature that was injured and in pain, a creature desperate for help. Far from being gross, it was something to be sheltered and protected. With one little breath, the bird went from being a *thing* to being a *being*.

How did my attitude toward the bird turn so suddenly? What caused the shift? The bird hadn't changed; only my perception of it had. The difference: I saw the life in it.

How often do we fail to see the life in other people? We do it with staggering frequency, every time we distance people from us by classifying them as other. On a macro level, we treat people as other when they are from a different country, or ethnicity, or religion, or region, or college, or political party. On a micro level, we dismiss individuals because they are weird, or poor, or ugly, or fat, or differently abled. It's easy to categorize people; we've been doing it since we were children choosing tables in the cafeteria at lunch.

But the more we wedge otherness between us and those we don't like or understand, the less humanity we see in them. This sense of otherness is the great chasm that still divides the LGBTQ community and the conservative church. By casting out queer Christians and the people who love them, the church has created a duality of in and out, a dividing line between those who are following God and those who, presumably, are misled. And the more barriers we put between us and another, the harder it is to see the light of the other person's spirit, the easier it is to see them as aberrant and abhorrent, and the easier it is to withhold our empathy.

What's the most common reaction of a person who has never seen two men kiss? *Gross.* Growing up as a kid in the 1980s, I heard it a thousand times. *Gross.* Is the only explanation for this visceral reaction that the act of two men kissing is inherently sinful and wrong? Or could it be that church and culture have created so much distance between themselves and the others that they are too far away to recognize a simple expression of love as anything but gross? When we disassociate ourselves from people, they stop being *beings* and become *things.* They are dead birds, worthy of nothing but a trash bin.

This is why we see our relationship as one small contribution to a larger mission. As the number of LGBTQ marriages in the world grows, that foreignness people feel toward queer couples will start to diminish. Normalization, however, is only the first step. The hard work in healing the divide is in getting to know those who would reject us and showing them our humanity. Someone can't be other when we're doing life together. Someone can't be gross when we've glimpsed the unfiltered, authentic humanity in them. This, of course, requires a willingness on both sides to see and be seen.

If only the church would look in the direction of LGBTQ people and watch them take a breath—see them kick and flutter, fighting for life in a hostile world. What a shift in perception the church would experience. Once we see the humanity in people, it's impossible to dismiss them as things. No person could be gross, for each is a living, breathing reflection of God.

It's important here to point out that progressive Christians also fall into the trap of labeling their conservative siblings as the other. Let us not extol ourselves as the nouveau righteous and dismiss those who for so long have dismissed us. If we hope for others to acknowledge our humanity, we must work to see theirs. Those on opposite ends of the theological spectrum or political aisle also flutter and kick in ways we may not see.

As for the actual bird, I contacted a local avian society and followed their instructions: I carefully scooped the bird into a box, then placed it beneath some shrubs for protection. The rest, they said, should be left to Mother Nature. The next time I passed that spot, the bird was gone. I wonder about it every time I go by, because I became invested in it—because for one moment in time we shared life together, and the heart doesn't easily forget.

Draw the Circle Wide

Whether you're single or married, perhaps you feel a mission to transform hearts and minds within the church. Perhaps you, like so many of us, have felt thwarted from the get-go. Maybe you've been rejected outright, sent scurrying away under a barrage of Bible passages. Or maybe you've been paid a lot of empty lip service through false smiles and evasive conversations. So many of us have faced church leaders more interested in posturing than in listening. They'll tell you all about the gospel of grace, but it doesn't feel as if they're living it.

How can we take a step in the direction of reconciliation when the outward face of Christianity is nothing but facade? The United States and many Western countries find themselves in an era when the hallmark of good faith is to posture about its importance and defend its virtue. Recent years have seen a string of Christian posturing: bathroom bills, religious freedom laws, anti-Muslim sentiments, zero tolerance for undocumented immigrants. This facade of Christianity claims to protect the fidelity of the religion, but its effect is to draw protective barriers that identify who is in and who is out.

Today's conservative church would rather *tell* the world about the love of Jesus than *show* any love themselves. The problem with this "telling Christianity" is that it becomes a religion about religion. It puts all of its energy in supporting the facade of faith rather than submitting to the life, death, and resurrection of Jesus. It becomes an empty husk. We admire and support family values and protections for children, but not when they become the rallying cries of a religion or, worse yet, walls designed to keep some people out. Our values should be an extension of our faith, not the measuring stick we use to determine who is a Christian and who is not.

Telling Christianity constitutes the laziest, most unsophisticated sort of faith. It draws neat lines with defined rules. It makes the Bible a reference book, with all answers easily accessible by finding the right passage. There is no critical thinking, because others have already done that for us, and there is no great mystery, because God is easily known and understood. It's comfortable faith. It's easy. It's inside the box. But how could we ever hope to fit God — the Alpha and the Omega (Christianity), the I Am That I Am (Judaism), the Perfection (Islam), the Supreme Soul (Hinduism) — inside a box?

Part of the reason we wanted to write about our marriage was to practice *showing Christianity*. In the midst of the Christian rules against same-sex unions and subsequent misperceptions about their inherently debauched nature, we wanted to offer our lives and our relationship as one example of what a gay union could actually look like. We wanted to invite people into the sloppy, imperfect experience of relationship and love, especially for those who have never witnessed a same-sex relationship up close. We've never been deeply engaged in activism, but more and more we see a calling to simply live by example and to show other Christians that godly same-sex union is possible by being (uncomfortably) open with our process. Our relationship is far from perfect; it suffers the same pitfalls and challenges of straight relationships. And we guess that's our point: to show others how normal it is.

What if we all became better *showing* Christians? What if we became more concerned with practicing our Christianity than with asserting it? It's harder than it sounds. Showing Christianity requires extending grace beyond which we are comfortable, loving in ways that are inconvenient, and acting sometimes in a manner that may be unpopular or misunderstood. It requires tearing down the walls that make our world so comfortably compartmentalized: gay-straight, Christian-Muslim, black-white, conservative-liberal, have-have not. It requires us to let go of the life preserver we know as rules and trust that God will buoy us regardless of where we drift in a boundless ocean.

"Show, don't tell" is a rule of good writing, and it has become a kind of mantra for us ever since we got married. We try to ask ourselves how we can show the people we encounter that we're people of faith without ever saying the words. It has caused us to think more critically about how we behave toward people and the choices we make. It has, in truth, revealed all sorts of ugliness in us. When our witness is stripped of Christian platitudes and justifications and is limited to simply how we treat other human beings, we're confronted with all of the subtle ways in which we ignore, belittle, and dehumanize others—especially those most in need of God's love.

The secular world would have a far more favorable view of Christianity if we were better at showing them the fruits of our faith than at telling them how they need to conform to belong. The Christian dialogue today would be less about creating laws to protect our faith and more about breaking down barriers to allow our love to spill out into the rest of the world. But that kind of approach requires a humility and vulnerability too many Christians aren't willing to express.

Let us draw the circle of inclusion ever wider. We're not talking about just the queer community or just faith communities—we're talking about all of humanity. LGBTQ Christians, who have had one foot inside the circle and one foot out, are uniquely positioned to bring about an epoch of reconciliation—not only between our community and the church, but between the church and the rest of the world. It's a mission that is nothing short of the work of heaven. It is nothing less than the continued work of Jesus to reunite a suffering world with the bound-less, bottomless, endless love of God.

Questions for Reflection

1. Do you believe marriages thrive on purpose and direc-tion? What purpose and direction does your relation-ship have?
2. Do you have an individual mission in life? How is that impacted or influenced by your relationship? How does it interplay with the mission of your relationship?
3. Do you believe LGBTQ marriages have a unique mission at this point in history? If so, what? Are all LGBTQ couples called to this?
4. How can the LGBTQ Christian community be better at showing Christianity when so much of the church is more concerned with posturing and "telling"?
5. How can LGBTQ Christians interact with the secular world in ways the traditional church may not be able to?
6. Most of us have experienced the feeling of being "other." Who do you treat as other in your life? How can you do better at seeing the humanity in them?

ACKNOWLEDGMENTS

Now that you've reached the end, we hope you share one of our takeaways: marriages flourish in community and whither in isolation. We could not have written this book—or ever have grown as a couple—without the wonderful, beloved community that surrounds us.

We're first of all grateful for the family members who support us, for the ways they've doubled down on love and relationship even when life has gotten rough. And we're grateful for Pearl Church in Portland, Oregon—the brave, loving Christian community that has fed our spirits and made the City of Roses feel like home.

We're grateful for our small group in Los Angeles—who saw our friendship grow and develop into a dating relationship—for loving us and accepting us even when we weren't sure dating was a good idea. Thank you, in particular, to David and Lehua for insisting on throwing us an engagement party even though we thought we didn't want one. We did, and your love touched us more than you know. We're grateful for our home groups in Portland, who saw us through our engagement and early stages of marriage—through stressful jobs and tight writing deadlines. And thank you, especially, Dan and Cheri, for loving us so well, for celebrating our marriage with a party we also initially said we didn't want.

To the Coppocks, the Roths, the Reeds, and the Duriases: Thank you for being both peers and confidants — for traveling with us on the glorious and uncertain path toward middle age, while blessing us with the wisdom you've gleaned from your decades' long marriages.

We're fortunate to have such good gay friends, whose group texts mean there's always a red notification dot on our messages app. Gabe, Ben, Matt, Andy, Jeremy: Keep blowing up our phones. And we're grateful for the Pearlers who have helped us grow in vulnerability through our monthly meetings: John, Ben, Nolan, Tom, Ryan, Brian, Jude, Mike. God bless you, brothers.

We want to acknowledge the friends we've made online — those we only see once or twice a year, and those we've never met in person but who nonetheless feel close. Thank you, GenEdge folks, for being our sounding board and providing a space where all can process questions of faith and sexuality. And thank you, Shane and the WUM Group, for always encouraging us and for the earnest manner in which you explore difficult questions.

Finally, a huge thank you to Rachel Held Evans, who generously took time out of a busy schedule — even with a newborn at home — to write a foreword for us, and to everyone who agreed to be interviewed for this project. And thank you to our editor, Jessica Miller Kelley, for taking a chance on us and helping us make this book a reality.

NOTES

―――――――――― CCO CO ――――――――――

Foreword

1. Alexander Schmemann, *For the Life of the World* (New York: St. Vladimir's Seminary Press, 1973), 89.

Chapter 1: Long Lines for the Tunnel of Love

1. Barry Schwartz, *The Paradox of Choice: Why More Is Less* (New York: Harper Perennial, 2005).

2. Brené Brown, *Daring Greatly* (New York: Avery Publishing, 2015), 8.

Chapter 2: The Journey through Uncertainty

1. Richard Rohr, "Trust the River," Center for Action and Contemplation, February 4, 2016, https://cac.org/trust-the-river-2016 -02-04.

2. Noel Ray, "How Christian Slaveholders Used the Bible to Justify Slavery," *Time*, February 23, 2018, http://time.com/5171819/ christianity-slavery-book-excerpt.

3. Benjamin Kaufman, "In Defense of the Need for Honest Dialogue," National Association for Research and Therapy of Homosexuality, August 5, 1999, http://web.archive.org/web/19990821 033023/http://narth.com:80/docs/indefense.html.

4. Joseph Campbell and Diane K. Osbon, *Reflections on the Art of Living: A Joseph Campbell Companion* (New York: HarperCollins, 1991), 18.

5. Blake Snyder, *Save the Cat!* (Studio City, CA: Michael Wiese Productions, 2005).

6. Maureen Stearns, *Conscious Courage: Turning Everyday Challenges into Opportunities* (Seminole, FL: Enrichment Books, 2004), 15.

7. "The Top Six Lessons I Learned from My M.O.M.," Modern Kinship, May 25, 2016, https://daveandtino.com/blog/2016/5/12/lessons frommom.

Chapter 3: Complications in Coupling

1. Andrew Belonsky, "Today in Gay History: *LA Law*'s Lesbian Kiss," *Out*, February 7, 2014, https://www.out.com/entertainment/today -gay-history/2014/02/05/la-law-lesbian-kiss-episode.

2. Keertana Sastry, "The Evolution of Television's Gay Kiss, from *Dawson's Creek* to *Rosanne*," *Bustle*, May 24, 2015, https://www .bustle.com/articles/85431-the-evolution-of-televisions-gay-kiss-from -dawsons-creek-to-rosanne.

3. Braden Goyette, "Omar Mateen Got 'Very Angry' Seeing Two Men Kissing, Father Tells NBC," *Los Angeles Times*, June 12, 2016, http://www.latimes.com/nation/la-na-orlando-nightclub-shooting-live -omar-mateen-got-very-angry-seeing-two-1465749495-htmlstory.html.

Chapter 4: Sex, Shame, and Spirituality

1. Michael Hobbes, "Together Alone: The Epidemic of Gay Loneliness," *Huffington Post*, March 2, 2017, https://highline.huffington post.com/articles/en/gay-loneliness.

2. Lily Dunn, "How I'm Overcoming Shame in My Sex Life," *Relevant*, March 10, 2015, https://relevantmagazine.com/life/relationships /how-im-overcoming-guilt-my-sex-life-update.

Chapter 8: Forsaking All Others

1. Carl Jung, *Psychology and Religion: West and East*, vol. 11 of *The Collected Works of C. G. Jung* (Princeton, NJ: Princeton University Press, 1938), 131.

Chapter 9: Who's the Wife?

1. James Brownson, *Bible, Gender, Sexuality: Reframing the Church's Debate on Same-Sex Relationships* (Grand Rapids: Wm. B. Eerdmans Publishing Co., 2013).

2. Ellie Lisitsa, "The Sound Relationship House: The Positive Perspective," Gottman Relationship Blog, November 28, 2012, https://www.gottman.com/blog/the-sound-relationship-house-the-positive-perspective.

3. Kyle Benson, "Emotionally Intelligent Husbands Are Key to a Lasting Marriage," Gottman Relationship Blog, October 7, 2016, https://www.gottman.com/blog/emotionally-intelligent-husbands-key-lasting-marriage.

4. Ellie Lisitsa, "The 12 Year Study," Gottman Relationship Blog, December 14, 2012, https://www.gottman.com/blog/the-12-year-study.

5. *Mary Ainsworth: Attachment and the Growth of Love*, directed by Davidson Films (San Luis Obispo, CA: Davidson Films, 2013).

6. Rachel S. F. Heller and Amir Levine, *Attached: The New Science of Adult Attachment and How It Can Help You Find—and Keep—Love* (New York: TarcherPerigee, 2012), 31.

7. Ibid., 29.

Chapter 10: On the Other Side of Vows

1. Stanley Kurtz, "What Is Wrong with Gay Marriage," *Commentary*, September 1, 2000, https://www.commentarymagazine.com/articles/what-is-wrong-with-gay-marriage.

2. John M. Gottman, "Observing Gay, Lesbian, and Heterosexual Couples' Relationships: Mathematical Modeling of Conflict Interaction," *Journal of Homosexuality* 45, no. 1 (2003), https://www.johngottman.net/wp-content/uploads/2011/05/Observing-Gay-Lesbian-and-heterosexual-Couples-Relationships-Mathematical-modeling-of-conflict-interactions.pdf.

3. John M. Gottman and Nan Silver, *The Seven Principles for Making Marriage Work* (New York: Harmony Books, 2015), 108.

4. Ibid., 14.

5. Ibid., 27.

6. See Gary Chapman, *The Five Love Languages: The Secret to Love That Lasts* (Chicago: Northfield Publishing, 2010).

Chapter 11: Intertwined in Intimacy

1. Rasheel Mushtaq, Sahil Mushtaq, Sheikh Shoib, and Tabindah Shah, "Relationship between Loneliness, Psychiatric Disorders, and Physical Health: A Review on the Psychological Aspects of Loneliness," U.S. National Library of Medicine National Institutes of Health, September 20, 2014, https://www.ncbi.nlm.nih.gov/pmc/articles /PMC4225959.

2. John M. Gottman and Nan Silver, *The Seven Principles for Making Marriage Work* (New York: Harmony Books, 2015), 71.

3. Ibid., 78–79.

4. Janice Wood, "Money Arguments Are Top Predictor of Divorce," PsychCentral, last modified October 6, 2015, https://psychcentral.com /news/2013/07/13/money-arguments-are-top-predictor-of-divorce /57147.html.

Chapter 12: A Long Business

1. *Downton Abbey*, season 2, episode 7, directed by James Strong, written by Julian Fellowes, BBC. United Kingdom, October 30, 2011.

Chapter 14: Relationship as Mission

1. Antoine de Saint-Exupéry, *Wind, Sand, and Stars* (New York: Harcourt, Brace & Co., 1939), 231.

2. Constantino Khalaf, "A Sanctuary for Humans, Part One," Zócalo Public Square, August 15, 2011, http://www.zocalo publicsquare.org/2011/08/15/a-sanctuary-for-humans-part-one/walk -like-an-american.